RV Flygirl

# RV Flygirl

## A Late Blooming Flygirl

Marcy Lange

iUniverse

**RV Flygirl**
**A Late Blooming Flygirl**

*iUniverse books may be ordered through booksellers or by contacting:*

*iUniverse*
*1663 Liberty Drive*
*Bloomington, IN 47403*
*www.iuniverse.com*
*1-800-Authors (1-800-288-4677)*

*ISBN: 978-1-4759-8850-5 (sc)*
*ISBN: 978-1-4759-8851-2 (e)*

*Library of Congress Control Number: 2013908959*

*Print information available on the last page.*

*iUniverse rev. date: 06/02/2015*

*Cover Photo By: Mark Sandstrom*
*Back Cover Photo By: Ellie Hussong*

# Contents

Acknowledgments............................................................ vii
Preface............................................................................ ix
Introduction—What Made Me Want to Fly ..................... xi

1. My Start in Flying ....................................................... 1
2. A Real Cross Country ................................................. 6
3. Soaring With Eagles ................................................ 20
4. The Flying-M Ranch ................................................ 24
5. Winter Winds ........................................................... 31
6. Young Eagle Teah ................................................... 36
7. RV Background ....................................................... 39
8. The Breakfast Bunch ............................................... 44
9. Oshkosh 2003 ........................................................ 46
10. A Gaggle of RVs ..................................................... 52
11. Best Trip Yet ........................................................... 54
12. Home Alone ............................................................ 58
13. Karly ....................................................................... 71
14. Jared ....................................................................... 74
15. Ralph ...................................................................... 77
16. Pancake Breakfast in Oshkosh ............................... 80
17. The Six State Sandwich ........................................... 82
18. A Hot Saturday In July ............................................ 89
19. 10 Minutes . . . Or Not............................................. 92

About the Author............................................................ 97

# Acknowledgments

Special thanks to my son Scott for the many hours he spent editing and his kind & encouraging words. Special thanks to Hank for introducing me to aviation and for his genius and skill in building airplanes. Special thanks to my friend Jake, who supplied me with additional RV history. And last but not least, thank you to the many RV pilots of Wisconsin and the Pacific Northwest who I've had the pleasure of meeting and flying with over the years. They have been kind, helpful, informative, and always willing to lend a hand to a fellow RV pilot. The aviation community has been a wonderful part of my life.

# Preface

*I* have flown small airplanes over America's mainland many times. I'm now an old woman who took up flying at fifty and have been traversing this amazing country ever since. Stressed, scared to tears, often without breath, and yet inwardly fulfilled—these are my experiences flying, memories that will forever remain vivid in my mind. The wonderful characters and people I've met along the way, the places and the planes, they're all planted firmly in my heart. So I've written these stories to help share my experiences with you . . . come fly with me!

# Introduction
# What Made Me Want to Fly

Growing up in Milwaukee, Wisconsin during the 'Happy Days' of the 1950's, I was a city girl who harbored no dreams of flying. High school graduation came and passed. At that time, I had dreams of being a lawyer, of getting a college education, of getting away from home. I enrolled at tiny Lakeland College in 1961, in rural farmland an hour north of Milwaukee, and started classes. After a while, life took on a different course. I would not complete college, learned the ways of farm life and, at nineteen, found myself in the role of homemaker and new mother, on a forty acre farm outside of Wausau, Wisconsin.

In the years that followed, much transpired that helped lead me to the aviating years of my life. First, I loved horses and was finally able to own one. Before long, one became four, and the herd increased further with the addition of sixteen other horses, animals 'boarded' on our farm by city residents without room for a horse.

Second, I learned to love the land and the freedom that living outside the city offered. You could say I have an adventurous heart. I loved gaming my horses and riding them like the wind. When my youngest child started school,

I went back to college and earned an Associate Degree in Mechanical Design. Transportation to these classes sparked my interest in motorcycles. We only had one car and to get to class, I needed an affordable option—thus, a motorcycle. Until a bad accident years later left me unable to ride any longer, I rode motorcycles.

And, thirdly, I became a small business owner. Developing my interest in photography, I started 'Action Images' in 1986, focusing on action sports and team photography. But it was the next step I took that further enhanced my interest in flying—aerial photography. Some local businesses became interested in aerial shots of their buildings and facilities layout, so I hired a local pilot and took my camera to the skies.

The beauty laid out beneath me was captivating and amazing. I saw my central Wisconsin home in a new light, with a changed perspective, and with a deeper appreciation for the features and lay of our land. Although I still had no dreams of being a pilot myself, subconsciously I think the seed had been planted. I was in the sky, I was seeing the country, and I was marveling the whole time. The only thing remaining was to grab the controls and fly the plane solo.

# My Start in Flying

*I*t was Hank that got me in an airplane and in the air, solo. Almost every aspect of my flying career is laced with reference and reliance upon him, as my best mentor and mechanic, my stubborn-minded but brilliant partner, in the air and on the ground.

About two years after my divorce, I went to a 'Singles Weekend,' organized around skiing, and was introduced to Hank. It was 1983. Everything we did was fast paced and exciting. There wasn't a slow bone in Hanks' body. We would marry years later, but until then, spent most of our free time together, laughing, dancing, skiing, motorcycling and enjoying each other.

While he was in the Air Force, Hank spent his free time as an airport bum, working hard to engage in anything related to aviating and planes, and this helped him to earn flying lessons. He had dreamed of airplanes and flying all his life. Now he was able to earn his way to a pilot's license. When he got out of the Air Force he worked in a machine shop and soon became the foreman. The plane-building seed was planted.

Dreaming of building his own airplane, he finally got started on one in 1969, in his garage. It wasn't long before Hank started his own business, working out of his garage evenings and weekends, doing small machining jobs. Soon, he bought some property just outside of Wausau and built a new machine shop, still working continuously to grow his business.

He loved building airplanes as much as he loved flying them. The first one was completed in 1970. I didn't know anything about airplanes when I met Hank and started flying with him, sometime in 1983, but I recall he was also building another plane too—the RV-4.

So for about ten years I flew with him, in his planes; first, the Davis Da-2A and then later, in his completed RV-4. I absolutely loved flying with him. It was always a thrill to see the world I knew from that bird's eye view. The perspective is so grand, so different. I was in the big, blue expanse above and it made me tingle.

The RV-4 is a tandem seating airplane, a taildragger; the third wheel is in the back of the airplane behind the main wheels, so the passenger rides behind the pilot. This is not my preference in seating arrangements because I like a clear view of what's ahead of me. Instead, I had to make do with the side views, which were still good. I was just happy to be along, and since I loved to fly with him, I went with him nearly all the time.

During this period, it never occurred to me to fly the airplane myself. While I was his passenger, I learned to read maps and understand the instruments, even though I could not see much of them without straining my neck. At times Hank would ask me to take the stick because he wanted to look at a map, so I'd take the stick and keep the airplane level, although the altitude would vary somewhat. The altimeter (displays the altitude) was located directly in front of Hank, so it was blocked from my view, which was a little frustrating. I felt I was flying blind.

Sometimes during our flights together we discussed instances where he had read about a pilot having a heart attack while flying. We'd wonder, 'what did a passenger do in that case?' It sort of worried me, thinking about that, because I did a lot of flying with him, as a passenger, and because we were both in our forties. I think he knew it worried me by all the questions I kept asking. So, soon afterwards, Hank gave me a gift certificate for an 'Introduction to Flying' course at our local airport. The certificate allowed me to attend a short ground school class and then, upon completion, to fly with the instructor.

That flight was in a J-5 Cub, a taildragger. I had nothing in front of me but the instrument panel. It was all right there! I could see everything! The J-5 Cub is a simple airplane, five-to-six instruments on the panel with a stick coming up out of the floor between your legs, for controlling the ailerons and pitch. Taildraggers are a little harder to land than a nose wheel or tri-gear (they have the third wheel in front of the main wheels), but when a student starts flying, they learn to land the taildragger soon enough, simply because that's what they're flying. It's not a requirement to learn the taildragger.

I had no idea what would happen on that instructional flight, or how it would change my life, but that definitely was the flight that changed me. The instructor, sitting behind me, would be in control. He did his pre-flight routine and talked of the steps ahead before we climbed into the Cub and took off. We were airborne. When we reached cruising altitude, he said to me, "Okay, the airplane's yours." He gave me complete control of the Cub. I took the stick and assumed command. I had the instruments in front of me, the Cub stayed level and steady, and I inhaled the moment for a brief second—I was flying! Within minutes, I was hooked.

I've asked myself, "Why, after 10 years of flying with Hank, did I suddenly want to fly the airplane myself?"

There were plenty of opportunities while flying with Hank to take the stick and fly the airplane, but I never requested to do that. I think the difference was in the seating—in the J-5 Cub, I sat in the front and actually felt like I was in control. I didn't feel that way sitting behind Hank in his RV-4.

I was enamored with flight. I immediately started taking lessons and soon soloed the J-5 Cub, on July 12, 1994. The Cub was the least expensive airplane to rent at our local airport, and it was a popular airplane because of that. After thirty-two hours of flying the Cub, and often having to wait in line to reserve it, I finally asked Hank one day, "Is there any reason I can't fly the old Davis airplane?"

The Davis was sitting in the back of his hangar at the airport, collecting dust. It had been parked there since Hank started flying the RV-4 several years earlier. Hank thought about it a few moments, scratched his head pensively, and said he didn't think that would be a problem. But he wanted to add ten inches to the wing tips to make the Davis more stable and perhaps easier for me to fly.

So he and a friend started the process of adding ten inches to the wing's length before I started taking lessons in the Davis. After thirty-two hours of instruction in the Cub, the Davis was a change. It was a zippy little airplane by comparison.

## The Davis DA-2A

We simply referred to it as 'The Davis.' Hank built it in 1968-1969, taking eighteen months to complete. It was built from plans designed by Leon Davis, or 'scratch built,' as they say in aviating circles. It cost only eighteen hundred dollars to build. Hank won the EAA Oshkosh Fly-In

'Craftsmanship Award' for The Davis and was selected for the cover photo of the June 1970 issue of *'Sport Aviation'* magazine. It cruised about 125 miles per hour (mph), had a used, top-overhauled 85 horsepower (hp) Continental engine, and burned 5-6 gallons per hour. Landing speeds were kept between 85 and 90 mph. It weighed seven-hundred and twenty-one pounds and made several trips to Texas in the 1970's and 1980's. There were over one hundred Davis airplanes built and flying during those years, when it was considered a sporty little airplane.

It handled like a dream, very light on the controls. Without flaps, the Davis had to be slowed by 'crabbing it' (tilting the airplane slightly sideways with the nose slightly up). Once landed, you had to keep the nose wheel up, with the tilt of the wing creating more drag to help slow it. I loved flying that airplane! I learned to fly it before I got my license and managed to put one-hundred hours on it before I officially received my pilots license. I had logged one hundred and thirty-two hours before I actually got my pilots license. I was just having too much fun flying that bird to get down to the serious business of getting the license.

The Davis could carry one passenger, if he or she were a light adult or a child. I generally flew it alone.

# A Real Cross Country

## August 1995

ate in May of 1995, at the age of 51, I became a private pilot. Hank had already moved out to the state of Oregon in February, ahead of me, as he was attempting to semi-retire and relocate one part of his business closer to his customers. His son would take over the rest of the business in central Wisconsin. I stayed back in Wisconsin to pack up our house, our furniture and belongings, and to finish my quest for a pilot's license. Officially, I'm a VFR Pilot (Visual Flight Rules), which means I can only fly when I have clear visibility. I'm not able to fly into the clouds.

It wasn't long before I moved on to Oregon as well, to join Hank. I tried to find someone to fly the Davis out to Oregon for me, but found it difficult to locate anyone willing to do that. A small plane soaring over big mountains (the Rockies) was a daunting proposition, so I wasn't surprised. I, too, was also leery. In my case, my inexperience flying in general and, specifically, zero flying experience over mountains, had me afraid initially to take on that challenge.

Whether I should fly the Davis to Oregon myself or not weighed heavy on my mind. But before I could think of flying west, I still had to take care of the moving details. We hired a moving truck in June, so the plan was to move everything from the house out to Oregon, come back to Wisconsin for the Annual Oshkosh Fly-In, and camp out there as usual. After Oshkosh, we would fly both airplanes, his RV-4 and the Davis, back to Oregon.

In July, Hank and I flew both airplanes into Oshkosh, Wisconsin (OSH) for the annual EAA Fly-In. (Every airport has a three digit identifier that can be a combination of letters and/or numbers. Oshkosh is an easy one—OSH.) That was my first experience flying solo into Oshkosh, although I had flown in there many times with Hank. Flying into Oshkosh alone, for a newly minted pilot, can be quite an experience. I vacillated between wonder and fright, excitement and terror, but my first solo flight into Oshkosh went without incident, primarily because we flew in early. In honor of this feat, I got a little name tag that said 'Oshkosh Pilot', a sticker for the airplane, and a mug.

Our plan for the long pending flight to Oregon was simple—I would lift off a day before Hank, meet him in Montana, and then we would fly over the mountains together. Sounds easy. His RV-4 cruised at 185 mph, the Davis at only 125 mph, top speed, so I would need the extra day simply to keep pace.

## Sunday, July 30, 1995

The weather forecast showed a storm heading toward Wisconsin. We had been watching the weather every day at Oshkosh, so we knew we'd get stuck in this storm at some point. My lift off was scheduled for early Sunday morning. The plan was to fly as far west as possible before the storm could hold me up. Oddly, it was a perfect morning for flying. By now I was resigned to making the flight—I just had to do it. I wasn't worried about many legs of this journey, but the Rocky Mountains worried me, no matter my efforts to curb the fears. Thankfully, though, I had a brand new Garmin 90 GPS to guide me, equipped with a moving map. With Sunday dawning, I took a short moment to glance at the skies, take in the weight of the flight I was about to embark on, and went airborne. The morning was clear, blue skies reigning, with only a few puffy, white clouds floating here and there. It was exhilarating to be nosing into that world again and I rose with only minor winds. At 3,000 feet, it was calm and I was on my way west.

Because of a back injury suffered in a motorcycle accident in 1986, I have trouble sitting for long periods of time. I get very stiff and the pain is bothersome. To help combat this, I planned to stop and stretch every two hours. My first stop was St. Cloud, Minnesota (STC), which should have only been a two hour flight. But the winds had picked up, so I climbed first to 4,500 feet, looking for lighter winds, then 6,500 feet. My ground speed had dwindled to 72 mph and I knew there would be stronger winds yet ahead, guiding the oncoming storm. But I wanted to complete that first leg. My back was hurting. I kept shifting my weight, as much as I could, to alleviate the pain. I was determined to make it to St. Cloud, and with the skies still clear, I faced no immediate flying danger. I simply had to deal with the winds and my back. Even experienced pilots bemoan the winds of the Midwest, which I was contending with as I got closer to St. Cloud and began my descent. They only got rougher.

When I entered the downwind at St. Cloud, I was scared to death. I bounced and bounced and bounced in the rough air. My landing there wasn't my best. I was very stressed, but after ballooning it twice, I finally got the Davis to touch down. It was as smooth a touchdown as I could have hoped for under these conditions.

I was elated to be on the ground safely, thankful for a very long runway. The winds at St. Cloud were thirty knots, gusting to thirty-five knots, but fortunately straight down the runway. The first two-hour leg ended up taking three hours. I could hardly stand up. I hobbled into the FBO (Fixed Base Operator or airport base) and called Hank to report in. After attending to my personal needs, I took a quiet moment to reflect and then called Flight Service. The weather forecast wasn't going to get any better that day, with the storm we had watched at Oshkosh moving in, the high winds leading the way. I knew I wouldn't be flying anymore that day.

After securing a room at a motel, I climbed into a steaming hot tub and soaked my weary bones. Thankfully, I had the evening to plan and rest up for the next legs of the trip. The weather was turning really nasty, sliding in overnight and showering St. Cloud with heavy rains. Thunder rumbled and lightning cracked throughout the night, so sleep was difficult.

## Monday, July 31, 1995

I awoke at daylight, but would be unable to fly until the weather cleared. A light rain still fell over the area and clouds socked in the airport, so I spent a leisurely morning hanging out at the St. Cloud airport. I called Flight Service several times that morning, inquiring into detailed flight conditions, and at about 11:00 a.m. they said there was a fifteen mile corridor in which I might be able to get through. But I'd have to find that corridor. I thought about that for a while, walked around outside, looked up at the sky, and contemplated doing what pilots have done many times—scud running. I'd call it 'flying through the crud,' a tactic somewhat dangerous because visibility is questionable and risks are raised. I've never done it myself before, but I've been along with Hank when he's done it, so I thought I'd go up and take a look around. I could always come back if I didn't like what I saw.

It was a cool morning. The airplane was ready and I was packed and ready to head west. I took off to take a look at the skies above. There was a portion of the sky to the southwest that was lighter than the rest, so I pointed the Davis towards the lighter sky. There was no wind at all. It was totally calm, so the flying was very smooth. It was serene up there; visibility was excellent, even though there wasn't even a hint of sun. I had been flying about twenty-five minutes and seemed to be getting closer to the lighter sky. My GPS was telling me I was way off course, but I knew that, and also where the closest airport was, in case I ran into trouble.

Suddenly there was rain on my windshield. It was a light rain, nothing to really worry about with a metal propeller (prop). The sky was a little lighter now, and I knew it wouldn't be long before I'd peek out of the scud. This light rain continued for about five-to-ten minutes, then stopped. Suddenly I was grabbing for my sunglasses. Walla! The sun! As I slowly corrected my course, the sun got hotter and brighter, and from that point forward it was calm, smooth flying. Now I felt confident that I could make it to the mountains. The storm we'd worried about so much was behind me.

Flying that second day was beautiful, even though it had started out with rain. The Davis was humming, the skies were clear, and I was going to cover some serious ground. My next pit stop was Jamestown, North Dakota (JMS), a leg of two-hundred and forty-one miles and what turned out to be 2.6 hours. A longer leg than I had planned, but it was smooth flying. Anyway, I was having more fun on a Monday than I'd ever had! The next stop would be Dickinson, North Dakota (DIK), only 2.1 hours through the air and one hundred and ninety-five ground miles. These legs were unfolding without much challenge.

My next leg, to Glendive, Montana (GDV), was short. About a half hour out of Dickenson (I was still tuned in to Dickenson on my radio), I heard Hank's voice calling in to GDV to land. I told him to call me on 122.75 after he landed. When he called in I acknowledged my position to him and he greeted me with, "Keep going, I'll catch up to you at Glendive." "Okay," I said. Dickenson to Glendive was only 1.1 hours in the air, and ninety-eight miles. My back was feeling the strain of flying for six hours already that day, but I had a feeling that once Hank caught up with me, he'd want to keep going. That's just the way he is.

I was right. When I landed at Glendive, I walked around the tarmac for a spell, limbering up and stretching out while waiting for him. I was wise to do that—Hank landed, gassed up, ran a restroom shift, and quickly hopped back into his RV-4. "Let's go!" he shouted, and we were off again.

Our next planned stop was Lewistown, Montana (LWT). It would be a long leg, but Lewiston is close to the point where we'd start the feared mountain legs of this journey. I was tired. I really wanted to quit for the day. I'd already flown over six hours and although the weather was cooperative, I was not accustomed to flying more than two-to-three hours in a single day.

Hank did not want to quit. He kept pushing. We landed at a little strip in Jordan, Montana (JDN), about one hundred miles from Glendive, just to take a break. There was nothing at that little airstrip—no gas, no people, no indoor restrooms. But they had an outhouse, which did come in handy. I took a few moments to enjoy stretching my back and legs and to smell the clear, crisp air. We walked around for nearly eight minutes total before climbing back into our planes and continuing on to Lewistown. As we got close, Hank commented over the plane's intercom that he'd like to make it as far as Stanford, Montana (S64) that night. He had been stranded in Stanford on one of his spring trips, and got to be friends with the FBO there. I tried to be understanding, I tried to hang in there, but I was already exhausted. I really didn't want to go that far. Still another forty miles! But I shifted my weight around again to relieve the growing discomfort and managed to keep myself, and the Davis, in the air. I would keep up with Hank and not let him down, and I would make it too.

Our leg from Glendive to Jordan to Stanford was two-hundred and fifty-seven ground miles, and 3.3 hours in the air. His friend was there to meet us and loan us his truck. Hank and I found a hamburger stand, then headed to his favorite motel in Montana—the 'Wayside Motel,' located at the end of the runway. My log book indicated I had been in the air 9.1 hours that day and my body felt like I had run a marathon. I was tired, very tired, and I will admit, crabby. So we didn't tear up the town that night, settling instead for Pepsi's at a relaxed pub and chatting with the local residents before calling it a night. More air miles tomorrow to rest up for.

## Tuesday, August 1, 1995

We were up Tuesday morning before daylight, my watch flashing 4:30 a.m. and my eyes straining to focus. The plan was to have coffee with Hanks' friend Mike, then depart for Rogers Pass. I was nervous. This was it. This was the part of the trip I'd been dreading. My first flight over the mountains in a small airplane was about four years ago, sitting behind Hank in the RV-4. I can easily recall the nerves I experienced then! Now I would be flying alone, in my small, twenty-five year old homebuilt Davis, high over these intimidating mountains. They did not look friendly, or easily conquered. Mountain flying is drastically different from the flying I was growing accustomed to in the Midwest. But it was a spectacular morning, the Big Sky country of Montana clear and baring a deep blue. Calm enveloped the day, now shaping up as a perfect day for flight. I wondered if the chill I felt was in the air, or was it in my psyche as I mentally approached the day? My pre-flight routine was extremely thorough—everything looked ready to go.

We climbed into our airplanes and headed for Roger's Pass. The RV-4 was in the lead and in true form, almost immediately racing ahead and vanishing from my sight. I had to keep telling Hank he was disappearing. It was still early and the winds hadn't picked up strength yet, so this leg of mountain flying would not be as bad as I had anticipated. I remember feeling quite relieved when we landed at Missoula, Montana (MSO) after 2.1 hours in the air and two-hundred and eight miles. It was 9:00 a.m. and we were both hungry, so Hank gassed up both airplanes while I went into the restaurant to order our breakfast. The food was fast and tasty, but we needed to get back up in the air. I remember feeling a little more confident heading forward, as we departed Missoula and headed up the Clark Fork River, to Sand Point, Idaho (SZT) and our next planned stop.

We climbed to an altitude of about 9,000 feet. The mountains around us were about 8,000 feet high, maybe more. I knew there was supposed to be a road somewhere beneath us, but I couldn't see anything but darkness below. At first it was only mild bumps and wind, but it didn't take long for the more serious winds to blow. I could have turned back, but I hung on. I didn't want to quit. My left hand was gripping the stick pretty tight and my knuckles were turning white. I remember the extra effort it took to lift my finger to press the radio switch, simply to talk to Hank. As before, he was racing ahead, quickly becoming a speck of black ahead of me. I think it was the sound of my crackling voice, my sniffling, my pleading with him to stay back with me, that finally got the message to him. He put his flaps down and began decreasing speed. I don't think he's ever flown at that altitude with the flaps down. The RV-4 engine does not run smooth when he slows it down to match my speed in the Davis, yet I needed him to do that because I absolutely needed to see that airplane ahead of me. I was scared, petrified like never before in my life. Tears were running down my cheeks. The sight of the RV-4 ahead of me was like a beacon in the night, my personal pacifier, even though I knew that if I got into any kind of trouble, he wouldn't be able to help at all. All he could do was talk to me over the radio. But seeing him, visually recognizing him, soothed my fears and allowed the flight to continue west.

The image of his RV-4 flying ahead, with the flaps down, is still in my head, along with the dark shadows of mountains below us. Hank talked to me, telling me it wouldn't be much further and we'd soon be there. "Relax, and just fly the airplane," he would say, continuing on with his soothing banter. I hung on fiercely to his words.

As Idaho stretched out underneath us, the sky was no longer as clear as it had been leaving Montana. It was getting grayer. Soon, Lake Pend lie just ahead. We began our descent for a landing at Sandpoint, Idaho.

Lake Pend is a very big, very long lake. At one time it had served as a submarine base, back in the days of World War II. I was feeling a little relief, thinking the worst was almost over, when it hit us. Major turbulence bounced us over the lake, my little Davis absorbing blow after blow, some subtle, some jarring. One blow jolted us especially hard. I almost lost it there, but recovered quickly and just hung on. I had learned something—I could 'tune-in' to my airplane. I could feel bumps coming milliseconds before they'd slap us and correct for them, somewhat reducing the jarring impact some of these gusts had. It required complete focus and serious concentration, but the advanced warning was worth the effort. Hank had asked me many times previously, since I had begun flying the Davis, if I felt like I was a part of it. I would always reply, "I don't know, what do you mean?" Now I know what he meant. There was a synergy between pilot and plane.

Sandpoint, Idaho was just ahead. As we approached traffic pattern altitude, I began believing I would live through this experience. The winds were blowing hard all the way into Sandpoint. Usually I quit flying when I've made a safe touchdown in these kind of conditions, and today my landing was fairly good, considering the turbulence. I felt a tremendous sense of relief while taxiing into the small FBO. Stepping out of the airplane, I was amazed at how lovely this setting was, how deep the blue skies were, and how mesmerizing the mountains were here, ringing this tiny airfield. But, my God, how the wind was blowing! Twenty-five knot winds gusting to forty knots on the ground—I could only imagine the wind speeds aloft!

I told Hank I didn't want to go back up today. It was too windy, and I really felt stressed. I had made it this far, I argued, and didn't want to go back up in the strong winds to push my luck and my abilities to the limit. I felt I had been a little lucky so far, but Hank was not happy about my protests. He is a seasoned pilot, and very competent, but also flies an RV-4 airplane that is about four hundred pounds heavier than my Davis. Although I trust his abilities and his judgment on nearly every occasion, I questioned his thinking here. I am not a seasoned pilot, have only been flying for one year, and only had about one hundred and thirty-five hours at the start of this trip, not to mention the far-lighter Davis I was flying. My fear and my instincts were telling me, 'Don't go back up there until the winds die down.' So I stood my ground and refused to fly in these winds. Finally, Hank agreed, and we hung out at the airport, waiting for the winds to die down. By four in the afternoon, it was still blowing with a fury, so we had to agree to call it a day. We'd get a motel room, a good night's sleep, and aim for an early start the next day.

## Wednesday, August 2, 1995

Wednesday morning, as I performed the pre-flight routine on the Davis, I patted the cowling gently, and whispered, "You've been a trusty little friend; take me the rest of the way to our new home." We lifted off from Sandpoint early, before 6 a.m., and took again to the skies, noses pointed west. As I reflected on our stop for a minute,

I thought, 'What an awesome place. Have to make it back sometime to Sandpoint.'

Our mountain flying was almost over. Once west of Sandpoint, it levels out fairly quickly and feels like the earth is slanting west to the Pacific Ocean. We were soon in Washington state, humming along nicely as we headed to our next destination, in Pasco, Washington (PSC). That leg was 1.7 hours and one hundred and eighty-five miles of smooth flying. We gassed the planes up, picked up some of 'Grandma's Cookies' and coffee for breakfast, and soon were on our way again. I was getting excited now—we would arrive at our new home today! The next stop was Hood River, Oregon (4S2), only 1.2 air hours and one hundred twenty-five ground miles away.

Hood River is enchanting! It was a sight I wanted to view through the lens of a camera, capturing the image forever. Absolutely stunning. A lush, elegant green carpeted the colorful hills surrounding this little town, it's cute little airstrip resting beside the great Columbia River. We landed there to get a weather briefing. We knew Portland was socked in—we could see very dark (almost black) clouds ahead. The hills bordering the Columbia Gorge were also cloaked with dark, ominous clouds that we would have to fly through to get to our new home. After waiting about two hours, Hank started to get antsy and wanted to scud-run through the Columbia Gorge, knowing the weather would be better in the Portland area. I was not so keen on doing that because the skies looked so threatening. He said, "Okay, you stay here and wait for it to lift. I'm going home, I've got work to do."

I really didn't want to be left behind, so I asked him if he'd fly with me through the Gorge. He wasn't happy about flying at my airspeed again, but finally agreed. So we lifted off and headed straight for the dark, massive clouds. I was terrified. Our altitude was 1,600 feet as we flew directly over the Columbia River. I think it was the unknown that scared me the most. The Columbia Gorge is huge, separating the states of Washington and Oregon and serving as the throughway for the great Columbia River, as it makes its way west to the Pacific. My little Davis would be a tiny speck in the Gorge, hardly visible at all. I remember seeing another aircraft flying on the other side of the Gorge, and it looked so tiny, so far away. When we finally got under the scud, I was amazed at how calm it was, how easy it was to fly, and how the visibility was good. That's not at all what I expected. We could see the ground clearly. But it was still scary up there above the river, the dark clouds completely encompassing us.

As I thought about what we were doing, I prayed. We had to stay under Portland's airspace, which would be no problem today, and as we approached Scappoose, Oregon (SPB), the sky was beginning to break up. We landed safely at Scappoose after 0.8 hours in the air and sixty-five miles. Scappoose will be where our airplanes call home, a mere six mile drive from our house. I climbed out of the Davis for the last time on this extraordinary cross country flight. I felt an incredible weight removed from my shoulders. It was over. I had made it!

The trip from Wausau, Wisconsin to Scappoose, Oregon totaled one thousand seven-hundred and sixty-five miles and 19.6 hours in the air, an average of 90 mph. I had made it and was proud—I flew a twenty-five year old, seven hundred and twenty-one pound home-built airplane nearly two thousand miles across America and the Rocky Mountains successfully. Although sometimes battered and bounced by the constant headwinds and pained from the long legs of flight, I patted the Davis again and thanked her for the ride. Her worth had been more than proven.

**"Davis DA-2A"**
**Photo by Ellie Hussong**

**"Hank's RV-4"**
**Photo By:  Marcy Lange**

# Soaring With Eagles

## August 1995

*I*t was a Saturday in August of 1995. What happened that Saturday helped establish what our future Saturday routines would be, not only with our RV's and Davis, but for many other RV's as well. Each of the other RV pilots we flew with in the Willamette Valley of Oregon had built their own RV's too, so on a Saturday morning our group of Oregon RV Pilots meet in the air at 7:30 a.m., tune our radios to 122.75, and communally decide where we'll fly for breakfast. I wasn't an RV pilot yet, and although the Davis is not in the same league with the RV's in airspeed, I was determined to fly it alongside the RV crew.

It was another sun-bathed morning in Oregon. We were itching to go flying. Hank was flying his RV-4, and I was flying the Davis. We were a little late getting the airplanes in the air, so when we tuned in to 122.75, there were no RVs on the frequency. We decided to fly down to Independence, Oregon (7S5), which has a nice, quaint restaurant called 'Annie's at the Airport'. On this morning, Hank told me to stay on course, that he was going to fly by his friend Jim's airstrip to see if they were there or gone. I stayed on course. Hank and I met Jim while living in Wisconsin. Jim was a commercial pilot for Northwest Airlines, based in Minneapolis, Minnesota at the time. After retiring, he moved out to Oregon and now lives on a small airstrip. Like Hank, Jim was an RV builder and a fun pilot to fly with—he was the first to 'roll' me in an RV (a slow roll on the horizontal axis).

About five minutes passed. Suddenly, I heard Jim's voice come over the radio. "Good morning, Hank," I heard him say. I heard Hank tell Jim that he and I were headed for Independence, and that I was supposed to be on course, flying the Davis. I was smiling as I listened to their chatter over the radio, when suddenly there was an airplane ahead of me, diving. It wasn't close enough to be a danger to me, but all I really saw was a shadow. I suspected it was an RV.

About a minute later, I sensed a presence off my right wing. Glancing over there, I was alarmed to see Dan (Jim's brother) flying his new RV-8 about three feet off my right wing tip! I took in a deep breath, and tried to stay calm. Then, in a heartbeat, I felt another presence, this one off to my left. I carefully glanced left, and immediately noticed another RV, also only about three feet off the tip of my left wing! I was sandwiched by RV's. This RV was being flown by Jim's daughter, Donna, in a RV-4. As I tried to take in the complete formation outside my Davis, I think I saw Jim flying his second RV-4 off Donna's wing tip, and only God knows where Hank was in his RV-4. Because I was unsure of his location, I didn't dare take my eyes or mind off my course—straight ahead. Having never flown in such close proximity to other planes before, I was extremely tense. Shaking-all-over scared. After several minutes I politely requested a little space, which they were quick to oblige, each plane retreating a little. However, even with the additional distance, I could still feel them on my side. I was still unnerved.

I've been in the back seat of Hanks' RV-4 when he's flown with some of his RV buddies in close formation, and that always made me a little nervous. There I was, flanked by RV's, leading the pack with my trusty little Davis. What a sight! My GPS indicated I was tracking about 108 mph, so the RVers all had to be throttling way back. When I noticed that my oil temperature wasn't indicating a reading, I started tapping the gauge with the palm of my right hand, which usually brings it up. Dan, still off my right wing tip, saw this and asked over the intercom, "What are you trying to do, make it go faster?" I laughed and explained that my oil temperature gauge often sticks.

We flew along like this for a while, the RVers chatting and comparing airspeeds, when Jim decided to pull out of formation and get some pictures. Hank quickly came up and took Jim's spot. I was nervous, but steady. Actually, at that point, I think I was more excited than nervous. Flying my tiny Davis with four RV's flanking me was a feeling I don't think I'll ever experience again. Donna, like Jim, is also a pilot for Northwest Airlines, and Dan is extremely important to the design of the RVs. They all have thousands of hours of flying under their belts, so it was really quite a thrill for me, less than three months a pilot, to be flying with these eagles of "Van's Air Force", as they were often called.

After about five more minutes of tight formation, Jim, Donna, and Dan decided to go on ahead. They peeled off and got into a three RV formation ahead of me, my eyes locked in as they began a series of rolls and dances and maneuvers that fascinated me. What an airshow! I felt privileged and honored, thankful I was a pilot and thankful for the personal display I witnessed. Amazing!

Van's Air Force, as the RVers of the Pacific Northwest were often referred to as, landed at Independence airport just a few minutes ahead of me. We all joined up for breakfast and talked the usual airplane talk, wrapping up another beautiful morning of flight. Eventually, I took off alone and headed home to Scappoose while Hank, Jim, Dan, and Donna went to look at RV projects (about 30) under construction there at the airfield. I spent the entire flight home reflecting on my latest thrill flying in Oregon, tired and worn but thankful.

**"Soaring With Eagles"**
**Photo by: Judy Van Grunsven**

# The Flying-M Ranch

## Fall 1995

*O*ur new home in Oregon was located in the foot hills of the Coastal Range of Mountains. To the east lie the Cascades. We are part of a lush valley that lies between the two ranges. The flying here is much different than the flying in Wisconsin, our old home. The view, wherever we fly here, is of mountains and foot hills and gorgeous green valleys. When I'm flying, I still think of the colorful farmlands of central Wisconsin, the patch work of crops and pasture and the varied colors they present. I miss seeing them, but being surrounded by such magnificence here certainly helps soften the loss. Besides, Oregon has a lot of farmland too, just not in the valley's we fly over. Eastern Oregon has many more crop fields.

But I digress. Hank took me in his RV-4 to the Flying M Ranch, because he wanted me to see this beautiful spot, and because he thought it was too dangerous for me to fly into. He wanted to first prepare me for the hazards and obstacles I'd encounter. The Flying M Ranch is nestled in a tiny valley within the vast Coastal Range, approximately forty miles east of the Pacific Ocean. We first flew over the ranch and circled it several times, Hank pointing out to me the layout and strategy for landing. After circling a final time, we began our descent. It was beautiful down there!

There were horses and cows and cabins, and a large, centralized log building that housed the ranch's restaurant and lodge. And there was a gravel runway. We skimmed the tree tops as we turned for final approach, but Hank had no trouble making the landing, which I acknowledged. This little valley was breath taking. The elevation at the Flying M is 448 feet, with the surrounding hills ranging from 2700 feet to 3425 feet. I'm guessing that the sun only shines on the ranch from mid-morning to mid-afternoon. The gravel runway is at the lowest point in the valley, 2100 feet long, with about 200 feet on one side, and maybe 150 feet on the other. This includes a parking lot for cars, and a parking area for airplanes. The valley is only about 2500 feet wide at its top, with rolling hills gracing each side. It is an awesome spot!

There were a half dozen other RV airplanes parked there waiting for us. The RV's had gaggled. This was my first glimpse of The Flying M Ranch, and I vowed to return.

## My Return and First Solo Flight Into the Flying M Ranch

Another Saturday dawned and we rose with the day, looking up to see only an azure blue with scattered fluff clouds decorating the skies. What a wide-open beauty Oregon offered! However, the plan that morning was to fly to Washington, to a small town called Packwood (55S) and a little airstrip there that featured a tasty breakfast cafe. Packwood is another awesome spot to fly into, located almost at the base of Mt. Rainier and just a little north of

Mt. St. Helens. Since I was planning to fly the Davis, which is a lot slower than Hanks' RV and the rest of the RV's we fly with, I lifted off at 7:00 a.m., instead of the usual 'wheels up' at 7:30. I always try to get a head start, so that I arrive at our destination before everyone is done eating.

By 7:20 I was north of the city of St. Helens, at 6000 feet, and coming up on Longview, Washington (KLS). My observations were that it was going to be near impossible to land in Packwood that morning. There was a thick layer of ground fog and clouds as far as I could see to the north and to the east.

Hank was lifting off from Scappoose about that time. As usual, we communicated on 122.75, where I discussed the situation with him. I kept my heading north towards Packwood, but soon there were a few more RV's squawking on 122.75, the RV pilots all discussing the dilemma briefly before deciding to go to The Flying M Ranch instead. I heard Hank's voice report in, "Well, uhhhh, uhhhh, Marcy's in the Davis, uhhhh, north of Longview, heading for Packwood. She lifted off early, and she's never flown the Davis into the Flying M." I'm sure everyone knew why I started out early. Because The Flying M Ranch is not located in the GPS memory banks, I tried to find it one day when I was out flying by myself, and couldn't, so I wondered now how I would be able to get there without assistance. Fortunately, I heard Bill volunteer to come find me, and lead me in. The Flying M is a good sixty-plus miles from where I was. As it turned out, Bill and his son Jeremy were flying the brand new RV-8 prototype that morning and more than happy to put their new plane to work. What an escort! It took Bill about ten minutes to catch up with me. I told him he could go play, or do some rolls or loops or something, because I know how slow he'd have to fly to stay back with me. I know Hank gets bored flying at my airspeed and I wanted Bill to still enjoy his new RV-8

Bill is a middle aged man who is very involved in the RV world. He is an RV builder and also a man who loves to fly. He's an easy going guy, friendly to all, with a kind word to say and always willing to lend a hand. Bill just throttled back and stayed along side of me, taking time to explain what I'd have to do to get into the Flying M. Some of the things he said that stuck in my head were, "You'll want to touch town by the water, and once you commit to final, there's no go around." Hank had said the same thing. He also added, "You don't have the power to pull up out of there, and you'll end up in the trees, or the side of the mountain."

Bill did the radio work for both airplanes. That was one less thing I'd have to do while attempting to land. We descended into what appeared to be a crevice in the mountain and approached from the southeast. I believe that's the only way to get in there, unless you're flying a helicopter. I got a glimpse of the ranch ahead of us. We entered the pattern upwind, descending, descending. 'Ya gotta do this right,' I told myself. 'You can always get this little Davis to loose altitude, just lower the wing and opposite rudder. It's simple, down, down, down more!'

Bill called in crosswind, and then left downwind. I glanced down at the runway as I crossed over it. Wow, it looked narrow! I saw the water Bill mentioned at the other end of the runway; it was only a tiny pond, but did serve well as a marker. 'Okay, I can do this,' I told myself. I had to drop one wing and hold the opposite rudder through most of the downwind, trying to lose altitude, and still Bill was much lower than I was. (The Davis has no flaps)

Bill banked sharply around a hill covered with good size pines. The hill just sticks up there and your only option is to go around it. He turned final, still descending fast. I could see he was using full flaps. I tried to see his touchdown point, but couldn't because I was concentrating on getting around this big bump without touching the tree tops, and trying to judge my altitude and distance in relationship to them. They are intimidating! I turned final a little too wide, the trees getting very close. I don't think I've ever turned that sharply. I was on final approach now, and I recall asking myself if I really wanted to do this. I had only a millisecond to think about it, and then the water whizzed by. I was committed now. I hadn't touched down yet. "Slow it down, slow it down, easy, easy, flare, flare, flare, hold it, hold it, make this good." (I talk to myself a lot when I need to concentrate. It helps me.) I needed to land the Davis at 90 mph. The main wheels touched, the nose wheel just barely touched, and I reached for the brakes, a right hand lever on the floor. This gravel was difficult to land on, painful and bumpy. I slowed down. I was finally on the ground, and I had used up every bit of the runway.

I taxied back looking for Hank. He stood with a bunch of RV pilots, all of them with eyes on me. There were a dozen RV's parked there. I cut the engine and simply sat there. I was trembling, my hands were shaking, but I knew I had executed it right, even though I used most of the runway. Bill came over to me, put his arm around my shoulder, and said I had done a nice job. That's Bill—he always has a kind word.

I felt good. I stepped out of the Davis, still shaking. Standing there, I tried to calm my nerves and steady my weak legs, looking around at the airport while Hank parked the Davis. It was a beautiful setting. The horses and cattle were grazing on an incline parallel to the runway and didn't seem bothered at all by the airplanes coming and going. It was so peaceful and serene. There was a shelter for the cattle attached to the hillside that I hadn't noticed from the air.

"Let's eat!" someone shouted, and we all headed into the big, rustic old lodge to get some grub.

After this landing experience and my safe arrival here at the Flying M Ranch, I wanted to relax, enjoy, savor the feeling of success. I couldn't quite do that. I tried, but I knew that I'd have to fly my Davis out of there yet today. You land from the east and take off to the east. There are no other options, no matter where the winds were blowing and no matter the speed. I was nervous. I did a short field take off, climbed steadily for what seemed an eternity, and soon found myself aloft again, clearing tree tops and hills and rising into the skies. No sweat. Getting out of there proved a lot easier than getting in.

I've flown into the Flying M Ranch many times in the three years I flew the Davis in Oregon. Once we had the RV-6A built and flying, I spent the next seven years going in and out of there. Each time was a pleasure. Each time it was beautiful and serene. Sometimes we'd fly there in the evening for dinner, flying out afterwards to watch the sun set behind the mountains. Then, turning for Scappoose, we'd land with the last hint of daylight. We were relaxed then, rewarding ourselves with the warm memory of another great day in the sky.

"Flying M Ranch"
**RVs parked in front of the Lodge**
**Photo by: Marcy Lange**

"Flying M Ranch"
**Photo by: Marcy Lange**

# Winter Winds

## December 1996

*I*t was another colorful, calm day in Oregon, about forty degrees with clear blue skies and a gentle crispness to the December air. A girl friend of mine, Kay, was also a fellow '99' pilot and today we planned on flying. (The '99s' is an organization of women pilots founded by Amelia Earhart and other noted female pilots of her era). Kay was a petite woman who was not only a pilot, but a Certified Flight Instructor, or CFI. She worked at an airport in Oregon and gave instruction to 'wannabe' pilots. She had logged several hundred more flight hours than I did but had never flown in a small homebuilt airplane. Kay and I had the day off from work and we planned to go flying in the Davis, assuming the weather would cooperate. We'd meet at the airport at 10:00 a.m., climb into the Davis and take off, destination Packwood, Washington, close to one hundred and ten miles northeast of Scappoose. Packwood is a beautiful spot nestled between mountains, almost at the foot of Mt. Rainier and just north of Mt. St. Helens. Mt. Adams is also close-by. I've been there four or five times, but Kay had never been there. I wanted to show it to her.

I arrived early at the airport. I did my preflight routine on the Davis and shut the hangar doors. All systems looked good. Soon Kay arrived and we departed Scappoose about 10:30 a.m. It was amazingly calm and warm in the sunlight at Scappoose. We couldn't have asked for a nicer day in December to go flying.

We decided to make a stop at Longview-Kelso airport nearby in Washington to visit Sara, another '99'er', and gas up. I've never flown into Kelso, although I have flown over it a dozen times. As we approached, the winds picked up. That's normal for Kelso. The Columbia River makes an eighty degree turn right there, with rising hills on either side. I got into the pattern and called in, recognizing that my base leg to final approach was very steep. The surrounding hillside didn't give me much choice. As I descended to short final the air evened out and we managed a smoother than expected landing. Sara, however, we missed. She had the day off.

With the gas tank full, we lifted off and continued our flight to Packwood. Yes, it was a gorgeous morning! Kay took over the controls and I began punching Packwood's coordinates into my GPS. I really enjoy flying with Kay. While she is flying I can enjoy more of the scenery and I can also play with the GPS. When I fly alone, I have to do it all, from flying the airplane and programming the GPS, to watching for traffic and checking the instruments constantly. Multi-tasking abilities are required. Sometimes I wish I had four hands to help me.

We headed toward Toledo, Washington, on our way to Packwood. There was a patch of ground fog hanging over Toledo and although we couldn't see the airport, we knew it was off my left shoulder. Now we were heading due east. There was more ground fog to the north, where Tacoma, Washington looked entirely fogged in, but to the east it was clear. The valley below us was still dressed in green. The north face of Mt. St. Helens came into clear view, off

Kay's one o'clock, a dark and intimidating edifice, although viewing it from the west and south, it is snowcapped and picturesque. It's interesting that ninety degrees can make such a difference. Mt. St. Helens erupted back in 1980 and being able to view it this day from the air was impressive. Many, many scars remain visible on the surrounding terrain from that tragic day.

Mt. Adams and Mt. Rainier were also in view, each with snow gracefully draping their shoulders. When Hank flies to Packwood, he flies right over the gaping hole in Mt. St. Helen's peak. That is the direct route to Packwood. I'm still more cautious when flying cross country, preferring to keep the roads and valleys below me.

We were coming up on Strom, a very small airstrip on the edge of the western Cascade Mountains. I wanted to show it to Kay. Hank told me to check out the small airstrips and know where they are, in case I ever ran into trouble. As we left the green valley and headed into the mountains, it began to get rough. I told Kay to head toward Strom. We had climbed to 4,000 feet, then another 500 feet, but it was still getting rougher. I was getting a little nervous. Kay has more hours and more ratings than I do, but I have more hours in the Davis. I took the stick and hoped Kay would understand. There was no time to talk. I was hanging onto that stick like there was no tomorrow, realizing there was no room to turn around. We had to make it through this little valley before we could even think about changing directions. I hung onto the stick firmly. We bounced and tipped and dropped a hundred feet at a time, only increasing our fears. I concentrated real hard on the feel of the airplane to counteract the bumping and bouncing. Kay didn't say anything. I think she was thinking the same thing I was. 'Let's get the heck out of here!'

It seemed like I'd been hanging on tightly for hours, but in reality I imagine it was maybe ten-to-twelve minutes. When we came to the opening, I simply announced that I was turning around. She didn't argue with me or say much at all. It was still rough going for a while, so I tried changing altitudes again, without success. It didn't matter. It remained rough until we got into the valley. Once we reached the green valleys again, the air seemed more docile. I breathed a sigh of relief, while Kay mentioned that her stomach didn't feel so good.

I pointed the Davis towards Scappoose. We could still go someplace for a sandwich, like Hillsboro, Oregon, just a hop away from Scappoose, and Kay nodded okay. The rest of our flight to Scappoose was, fortunately, smooth. We flew over the airfield at 1800 feet and kept our heading to Hillsboro. The windsock was calm, typical at Scappoose. However, as we were coming up on Cornelius Pass, I noticed a large dot in the sky to my left. I kept watching it and sure enough, it was coming right at us! I kept watching and saw its path was only slightly higher than ours. It was a commercial airliner that had just taken off from Portland, but its flight path was unusual. I don't think we were even seen. It kept plowing forward into the sky, started turning left, and then continued its climb. If I turned to the left, I would surely get caught in the wake turbulence. If I turned right, a hill. Although I tried veering quickly to the right initially, I knew we were going to be caught in the turbulence. There was no way out. Grip the stick tightly and pray, I told myself. I did both as the ride became extremely rough. I hung on for dear life and waited for the pounding to stop. Glancing out my left window, I was surprised to see yet another airliner passing overhead. No wonder we were bouncing so much!

This turbulence battle kept me so busy I didn't have time to punch in the Hillsboro frequency. I nudged Kay, asking if she could get Hillsboro on the radio. By the time I could take a second to press the switch to talk to Hillsboro, we were almost on top of the airport. And that's a scary thought. Hillsboro is a busy airport. I told them where we were and our altitude and that I was trying my best to keep the airplane in the air. The controller asked if I was going to land. I told her I was trying to keep the airplane in the air, and then I'd turn it around and head back to Scappoose. I don't think she understood, but I'm sure she could see us and hopefully would keep other aircraft away from us.

When we got back over the pass and into the Scappoose valley, the air was calm again. I shook my shoulders and neck to loosen up. I glanced over at Kay. Her face was the color of a freshly washed white sheet, and she was leaning into my tiny little air vent with her hands cupped, trying to scoop up as much of the fresh air as possible. I was so busy with the airplane I hadn't even noticed how she was dealing with the turbulence. How insensitive of me! I have never been airsick or seasick. I told her to hang on, we were almost back.

My landing at Scappoose was smooth. We taxied up to the fuel pump and got out. Kay walked around and soon got some color back. She said she'd never been airsick before, and didn't like it much. She's got a lot of hours flying, so I was really surprised she got sick.

We flew 2.25 hours that morning, did not get our lunch, and were only a little worse for wear. Perhaps we'll try Packwood again, next summer, when the wind or some airliner isn't trying to blow us out of the sky. When I got home and told Hank about our flying experience, he said, "Well, did you learn something about winter flying in the mountains?" We certainly had.

# Young Eagle Teah

*T*he Young Eagles Program is sponsored by EAA Headquarters in Oshkosh. Pilots who are members of EAA volunteer their time and their airplanes to give airplane rides to children, free of charge. The parent must give written permission on EAA forms and after the child's flight his/her name is entered into the world's largest logbook at EAA Headquarters. The purpose of this program is to give children the positive experience of flight.

I became involved in the Young Eagles Program in the early 1990's, at the program's beginning. At that time I was not yet flying. However, there was always a place for non-pilots to participate and I became very involved with our local EAA Chapter, organizing and coordinating the Young Eagles Flight Rally's we held at several different airports in central Wisconsin. This involvement came with the title, 'Ground Crew Chief'. I always enjoyed being involved with the aviation activities. I remember vividly a day we had a Young Eagle Rally in Antigo, Wisconsin. I was Ground Grew Chief and Hank was there to give airplane rides in his RV-4. That day we gave rides to over 200 children and Hank alone gave rides to twenty of them, one at a time, in his RV-4. I was exhausted at the end of the day, and so was Hank.

After I became a pilot and had experienced about two-hundred and fifty hours of safe flying, I wanted to start flying Young Eagles too.

My very first and most memorable Young Eagle Flight was with the seven year old granddaughter of my neighbor. Her name was Teah and she had never been flying. She was a cute girl, with long dark hair and the brightest eyes. She was anxious to get in my little Davis. I walked her around the plane, explaining the pre-flight routine to her as best as I could, at a level she could understand. I was new to this aspect of Young Eagles. She seemed to understand everything, which surprised me. So we got in the Davis excitedly and buckled up. I started the engine and taxied to the run-up area. I kept glancing at her through the corner of my eye to try to read her. I'd been around pilots for many years who gave Young Eagle rides, so I'd heard all kinds of stories about the Young Eagle being scared, or sick, or nervous, so I watched her closely.

When I asked her if she was ready, she shook her head up and down with the broadest grin on her face. I taxied to the threshold, glanced over at her once more and went to full power. She was leaning forward in the seat beside me, stretching her neck to see as much as she could. With the Davis being a low wing airplane and Teah being so small, she had to stretch to see more. She was looking out the window as we gained speed. I lifted off and as we got to forty or fifty feet above ground level she was still leaning forward, looking outside and down at the ground below us. "Cool, this is really cool!" She yelled at me excitedly, but it was sure loud in the headphones we were wearing to communicate with. I thought my eardrums would burst! I smiled and felt a warm glow inside. This little girl was really having fun. She was excited and wide-eyed, looking everywhere to take it all in.

Teah was only seven years old! I told her I'd show her Grandma's house, so I turned the Davis in that direction. When we were about two miles from her Grandma's house, at about 1500 feet, I heard her shout, "I see it! I see Grandma's house! It's right there!" She pointed to it. I couldn't see her Grandma's house yet, but she was definitely pointing in the right direction. I wasn't sure she really could see her Grandma's house, until we got closer. She was right on target. "They're playing in the backyard!" she yelled. I couldn't believe it. Grandma's house is a ranch house, not a real big one, but she definitely saw it. I asked her if she wanted to see anything else, and she wanted to see the race track, where her daddy raced cars. I knew it was in the city of St. Helen's, but I'd never been there, so I told her to look for it because I didn't know where it was. I pointed the nose of the Davis towards St. Helens, figuring I'd be able to spot a race track, but she picked out that race track right off. Seven years old.

We flew around for a while. I circled the track and then the city of St. Helens, pointing out the schools. I asked her if she knew how to get back to the airport. She turned around and pointed behind us and said, "It's there, over there!" She was right. She has a great sense of orientation, has absolutely no fear of flying, and was a pure joy to have sitting next to me.

I've thought about her many times since. She was a little girl who should be exposed to aviation, she seemed so at home in the airplane and in the skies. Someone will have to do it, so I look forward to keeping her eyes open to the possibility.

Most of the Young Eagle Flights are not as memorable or as exciting as the ones I had with Teah. It only takes one or two like her to make it a tremendously rewarding experience.

# RV Background

*I*n September of 1997, Hank picked up a fast build RV-6A kit, (the fast build kit has the fuselage partially built and the wings partially built) from Van's Aircraft in Oregon. For ten months he worked steadily, after work and on weekends, building the RV-6A. I was there doing a lot of the grunt work and errands required in the building process, but Hank is a genius when building an airplane. On July 2$^{nd}$, 1998 he took the 6A for its maiden flight. Three weeks later he flew it with me sitting right seat to Oshkosh, Wisconsin for the annual EAA Fly-In. It took me many months and lots of hours of dual flight before I began flying the 6A solo. We both loved flying the RV-6A and I believe we managed to put over three hundred hours on the 6A in a little over a year.

Soon after I took over the stick of the 6A, Hank decided to build another airplane, the RV-8A. He flew it for the first time in November of 2002. From that time on we flew the 8A and the 6A everywhere.

The rest of my stories revolve around my flights in the RV-6A. I truly love flying the 6A. It is a beautifully designed and efficiently built airplane. I call it 'sweetheart' sometimes, because it is such a sweetheart to fly. It has carried me thousands and thousands of miles, purring like a lap cat over them all.

To give you a little insight and background into the RV's, I've included the following summary:

'**RV**' originated from the initials of the designer, **R**ichard **V**an Grunsven, who is the designer of the all-aluminum series of RV aircraft. His nickname is 'Van', thus the company name, Van's Aircraft, Inc. All RV's are classified and licensed in the experimental category by the Federal Aviation Administration (FAA) and are 'homebuilts' or 'experimentals'. The model designation, starting with the RV-3, have generally been numbered sequentially in the order each model was designed. The number following the dash actually denotes the model, and an 'A' following the model designation usually means that model has a nose wheel. Normally the straight number indicates the design has a tail wheel. The exception to that format is that the RV-10 and RV-12 are only available with a nose wheel. All RV's are low wing aircraft.

The first model that was available as a 'kit' was a single-seat taildragger aircraft, called the RV-3. It was introduced to the public in the early 1970s. I say 'kit' because there were several prior aircraft that Van modified before he designed the clean-sheet RV-3. A 'kit' consists of all the pieces, machine fabricated parts, including aluminum sheets, plus required weldments and fasteners that the homebuilder assembles in a garage, basement or in some instances in the builders living room or bedroom. (That's another story).

Shortly after the RV-3, homebuilt aircraft were being completed and flown around the country with previously unrecognized levels of performance. Soon there was a cry from pilots for a 2-place model with similar performance. Van went back to the drawing board to develop a new tandem design, the RV-4, that would accommodate a passenger. The RV-4 was introduced to the public in 1979, with kit parts available shortly thereafter. Kit sales kept increasing, but now pilots wanted to have a model where the passenger sat next to the pilot, rather than behind, and Van again went back to the drawing board and designed a side-by-side model he called the RV-6. The RV-6 was the first with a side-by-side seating arrangement. Again, it was a taildragger and could carry a single passenger.

Shortly after the RV-6, the RV-6A variant was made available. These became available in the late 1980's. There was an RV-5 designed that was not brought to market. Within a few years, there were a few hundred RV-4's flying. That alone is an amazing fact, since at that time they were all built from basic kit parts, or scratch built. Later, partially assembled kits, called 'quick build kits' were made available to speed the building process for most models. The quick build option was enabled due to the partial assembly process undertaken by a company in the Philippines, where lower labor costs and good workmanship provided a lot of hours of labor at a low cost.

A kit can be partially assembled commercially, but the homebuilder must complete at least 51% to satisfy the FAA experimental homebuilder rules. A quick-build option costs slightly more but will save the builder one or more years of construction time.

A lot of pilots prefer the tandem seating arrangement. The designer, Van, always listening to his customers, came out with a design around 1994-95 that was similar to the RV-4, only it was a lot roomier inside. That new design was called the RV-8, or as they say, "The RV-8 is a fat 4." It looks like the RV-4, but it's bigger, a lot roomier, and can carry more luggage, and I believe the RV-8's have more speed. That, however, may be directly related to the engine type, since all the RV's sport an aerodynamic design

41

ensuring speed. Anyway, as human nature seems to always dictate the need for more, or better choices, the designer again listened to his customers, and the nose wheel version of the RV-8 was born and tagged the RV-8A.

The next RV to come online was designed to be a 'trainer' airplane. It is the RV-9A, which is a side-by-side seating, one passenger nose wheel airplane. It has a longer wing and a slower stall speed (40 mph). Up to this point, it is the only RV that is not capable of light aerobatics.

The next airplane to come online was the RV-7 and the RV-7A, which are identical to the RV-6 and RV-6A and have literally replaced the 6's. The differences are only noticed in the building process. They look the same, and perform the same, but the building process is easier.

The next online is the RV-10. The advertising for this model says, 'The Perfect 10,' and it was a request from builders since the late 1990's, finally coming out several years ago. The RV-10 is a 4-passenger airplane and comes only as a nose wheel model.

In early 2000's, a new category of aircraft was approved by the FAA, called Light Sport Aircraft (LSA). The LSA rules restrict the maximum gross weight of aircraft built under this classification, as well as setting the maximum cruise speed at 138 mph. This classification of pilots must have a pilot's license, but a medical certificate issued by an FAA-approved doctor is not needed. A pilot flying under LSA rules is required to self-certify oneself that they are fit to fly. To meet this need, Van's Aircraft designed the RV-12, built under the standards and specifications established by the American Society for Testing and Materials (ASTM).

The RV-12 was followed by a new larger side-by-side model to accommodate larger people, called the RV-14.

As of this printing there are over 8000 RV's flying between all countries around the world, wherever private aviation is permitted.

The designer, Richard Van Grunsven, is an amazing man. He always keeps economy for the customer forefront in all his design decisions. The kits sell for an amazingly low price, starting under twenty thousand dollars. The builder adds the engine and instruments, which are also available for purchase from Van's Aircraft. If you've ever shopped around for kit built airplanes, you would soon come to the conclusion that the RV is the highest performing, most economical airplane to operate at the lowest price.

I can testify that the RV is an amazing airplane to fly cross country. Burning about five-to-seven gallons an hour at cruise, you can easily travel 180-200 miles in an hour, and often more than that. So when you compare that to an airplane that only burns five gals an hour and travels 100 mph, which airplane is more economical? On one particular trip, three RV airplanes, my RV-6A, Hanks' RV-8A, and an RV-6, flew from the Portland area to Oshkosh in just under nine hours, which is a distance of roughly 1900 air miles. Although that was the shortest trip we ever made, the trips were routinely between nine and eleven hours. Granted, the trips from west to east were always shorter, due to slight tailwinds. The trips back to Oregon, however, east to west, were typically between ten and fourteen hours. I don't recall a trip from Wisconsin to Oregon in the ten years that I made them that we didn't have to deviate from our route because of weather. For some reason the trips west bound were always burdened with weather issues. On one particular trip I almost ended up in Canada because of foul weather. I was flying alone on that trip.

# The Breakfast Bunch

## May 2003

*B*eing a member of EAA and, specifically, EAA Chapter 105, in addition to flying the RV, has been an experience to treasure. I'm not sure I've had other experiences that can compare. Since moving to Oregon in 1995, Saturday mornings were for flying. The routine was wheels up at 7:30 a.m. and tune in to radio frequency 122.75. You say, "Any RV's up this morning?" And the chatter begins. "Where are we going for breakfast?" You will see anywhere from three to four to as many as ten to fifteen RV's flying into a favorite spot for breakfast. I can't remember a time when it was just Hank and I.

On Saturday, the 31st of May, Hank and I went to the airport to get our airplanes ready to fly. We were a little early (wheels were up at 7:00 a.m.), so we got a head start on the rendezvous time of 7:30. There were no RV's on the radio yet and we decided to head south towards Independence, thinking if nobody else got up, we'd get breakfast there. We were flying at about 2000 feet, with low ceilings and patches of darker, gray clouds all around us, normal weather conditions for winter in Oregon. It threatens to rain a lot, but usually holds off. Temperatures were in the upper forties and the winds were calm, making for an enjoyable flight. There was no real weather threat facing us.

We were almost to Salem, Oregon when other RV pilots came on the air. The discussion that followed led us to point our planes again towards The Flying M Ranch. I was the first one to land, and very thankful I'd gotten a head start that day. My landing left a lot to be desired, although it wasn't a hard landing. I was relieved to see the other RV pilots weren't all standing along the runway watching, as is often the case. Most days, I'm the only woman along with the guys and always the only woman flying an RV. Sometimes it's intimidating having all these fellow pilots observing my landing techniques and flying style, but generally they've always been welcoming and supportive of me.

This particular Saturday morning there were eleven RV's flying into the Flying M. Of course the chatter was the same—fuel burns, oil temperatures, cylinder head temperatures, who flew here or there—but always the usual camaraderie. We had a delicious breakfast and headed back home with the ceilings still low, but no rain.

We did a lot of flying in cloudy weather. It threatened to rain a lot, but the rains were not heavy or torrential like they are in the Midwest. Winter months we often flew in overcast skies and never experienced a drop of rain. And it was usually extremely calm in those conditions. Back in the Midwest, you wouldn't think of going flying with those overcast skies.

# Oshkosh 2003

For those of you who have flown across the country to attend the annual 'Fly-In' at Oshkosh each July, now tagged 'AirVenture', you're familiar with all the preparations and planning that takes place beforehand. For Hank and I, the trip is not only an adventure we look forward to each year, but also a 'going home'. Our roots are in Wisconsin, with both family and friends still living throughout the state. Generally, we plan on taking both airplanes, the RV-6A and now the new RV-8A. Getting two airplanes ready for the cross country flight is a lot of work, so the month of July is an extremely busy and hectic time. Attendance at the fly-in is our primary goal, but we also look forward to seeing family and old friends. Our campground at Oshkosh is surrounded by many of these old friends and evenings are spent there visiting and catching up.

The trip is always more fun when there are a couple airplanes flying together, and this year Joe flew with us in his brand new RV-9A, along with his Australian friend, Ivan. Hank and I were each flying solo, which meant we had some extra room for some of Joe and Ivan's luggage.

The plan was to lift off about 6:00 a.m. on the 24th of July. Since Joe lives seventy miles south, he was going to lift off about ten minutes before us and meet us in-air, probably somewhere in eastern Oregon. Aside from being a good friend, Joe's a great guy to have along on any trip because he's good company and a knowledgeable man to talk with, and also because he surfs the Web and finds the best fuel prices along our route. Joe is tall and thin, wears glasses and has grey hair. He's very goal-orientated and once he starts a project, he works steadily to complete it. He's always willing to help his friends and neighbors, especially if it involves airplanes, although he also enjoys working on cars. Joe has built 2 RVs and has helped re-build a number of other RVs with friends. His wife also enjoys flying and is occasionally with him on our breakfast fly-outs.

Our lift off was about ten minutes late, but we did meet Joe and Ivan in the air a little east of the Columbia Gorge. The three RV's have the exact same engine, the only difference being that Hank has the FADEC engine configuration in his 8A. Hank started in the lead, but I was constantly adjusting my speed to his 'automatic' engine. About an hour into the flight, Joe took the lead with his 9A. That seemed to work out better, so Joe and Ivan held the lead the rest of the trip. We were Wisconsin-bound.

We landed at Helena, Montana (HLN) at 9:00 a.m., the first leg being roughly 2.8 hours. We fueled up, had breakfast, and by the time we got back to the airplanes, the temperature had soared to ninety-six degrees. Jim was right—fuel was cheap there, at $2.19 per gallon. All three airplanes burned about twenty-one gallons of gas, plus or minus a couple tenths of a gallon.

Our next leg started at 10:25 a.m. and the heat was suffocating. Ordinarily I wouldn't fly in temperatures this hot, but we were on a mission and the heat would not be relenting any time soon. We tried to climb out of the heat and managed to find slightly cooler air at 11,500 feet. We were heading for Mandan, North Dakota (Y19) and arrived there in 2.85 hours, or 1:20 p.m. Pacific Standard Time (PST), in temperatures still steady at ninety-eight degrees. We'd flown 5.75 hours that day, in blistering heat, and were exhausted, although I appeared to be the only one willing to admit that. But I knew they were worn out too, because not one of the three complained about stopping for the day. We all fueled up, compared our fuel burn, and again noticed the burn was very close, within a few tenths of a gallon. The price of gas in Mandan was $1.99 per gallon.

The FBO at Mandan was a prince. He waited for us at the end of the runway, with his car running and the air conditioning on, as we tied down the airplanes, hauled out our overnight stuff, and put canopy covers on the airplanes. We were all sweating heavily by the time we crawled into his car, the cool air inside like a slap of refreshment for our overheated foursome. He took us to a nice Best Western in town and helped carry in our luggage, telling us also a little about his wife and three young kids while we talked a little about airplanes. I wanted to give him some money to take his kids out for ice cream, but of course he refused.

Our hotel was suitable, the best part of course being the air conditioning was working. After we cooled off a bit, showered and took a nap, we went down to the restaurant for dinner. There was even live music there. Of course the dinner talk was all airplanes. By the end of the day, I'd like a little variety in conversation and it's then I often wish there was another woman along. I can listen only so long to conversations centered on engines, oils, additives, fuel burns, air speeds, and props, without missing the more familiar subjects of home and family, books and movies, even shopping—and I'm not a big shopper!

We planned to lift off early the following morning, primarily to beat the heat. I'm convinced that Hank's second middle name is 'Early' (his first middle name is 'Hurry'), so we were at the airport pre-dawn and as is customary, had to wait for the other two pilots to arrive. I call this the 'hurry up and wait' syndrome. We finally managed to lift off at 6:37 a.m. Central Standard Time (CST). There was a thin layer of fog moving in and ten minutes later Mandan was Instrument Flight Rules (IFR) only, so thanks to Hank's middle names, we got out of Mandan just before it got fogged in. Whew—we were on our way again!.

That morning flight was pleasant, with only twenty minutes of bumps we encountered while flying between two weather fronts. After getting past the fronts, the air again evened out and it was as smooth as glass thereafter.

There was the usual chatter along the way, but we held it steady, pointing the noses east. Hank and I had been awake since 4:30 a.m. and were beginning to get hungry. Knowing we'd arrive at Oshkosh two days before 'AirVenture' actually began, we also knew there would be no food booths open for business yet. We didn't have a car or transportation awaiting us there either, so I suggested we deviate our heading slightly and land at the Central Wisconsin Airport (CWA), near Wausau. It's a towered field that has a restaurant we've eaten at many times before, so the others agreed and we headed that way.

CWA is also where I practiced my towered field landings when I was learning to fly. Back then, there was very little traffic at CWA and when I flew down there to practice, I'd tell them I was a student pilot and they would go out of their way to help. So our detour this morning was something akin to 'going home.' I even offered to do the radio work for our flight of three RV's, but soon learned that was a mistake!

I called in our flight of three RV's about twenty miles out from CWA. I was excited to have arrived in my old flying neighborhood and began talking to the tower, but the controller sounded young and a bit confused. Perhaps he didn't know what RV's were, or perhaps he'd never landed three airplanes together. Anyway, the radio communications were so confusing and disjointed that Hank got very frustrated, deciding to leave our flight pattern, circle, and come back in on his own. CWA is a great airport, with perhaps a dozen or two commercial flights coming and going in a day. It has very wide, long runways, is towered and has virtually no traffic. I think little Independence, Oregon has more traffic per day than CWA. Anyway, despite the radio confusion, we all made it in to CWA safely, landing at 9:37 a.m. CST and finally completing a 3.0 hour leg. We secured our airplanes and headed for the restaurant.

We had a delicious breakfast, but I was restless. I was only twenty minutes away now from my family and friends, and I had just accomplished a trip that always leaves me feeling 'high.' Anyway, I went downstairs to the car rental places and asked about renting a car. They didn't have any medium or full size cars left; in fact, the gal said all they had left was a Lincoln Continental. So I said to her, "Well, then, you'll rent me the Lincoln for the price of a mid-size, right?" She looked at me, thought about it, and said, "Okay, I can do that." I was elated. We had wheels. The only problem was that I couldn't fly the airplane and drive the car at the same time, so we decided to park the RV-6A at CWA. The FBO there was a real nice gal and promised to keep a sharp eye on it. We secured the 6A, then unloaded all of our luggage into the Lincoln. CWA is about a thirty minute flight northwest of Oshkosh, and about a 1.5 hour drive. The guys would fly in and set up camp while I drove the luggage down from CWA.

Our total flying time for the cross country flight—Scappoose, Oregon to Central Wisconsin Airport, Wisconsin—was 8 hours and 45 minutes. If we wouldn't have detoured to CWA, the flight time from Scappoose to Oshkosh would also have been 8 hours and 45 minutes. Yes, we could have made the flight all in one day, if the weather was good, but with temperatures soaring we were wiser to break the trip up into two days of flying. This way we'd avoid being totally exhausted by the time we arrived in Oshkosh.

**"Hank's RV-8A"**
**Photo by: Marcy Lange**

# A Gaggle of RVs

## How many RVs does it take to fly 16 people to breakfast?

I t was a dreary Saturday morning, one of many we've had this spring. However, it was a Saturday, and we were die-hard pilots not willing to so easily give up a fly day. We were still eager to go. We did our usual wheels up at 7:30 a.m., met in the air on 122.75, and then decided where to go. Hank and I were wheels up a little early, about 7:20 a.m., from our home airport in Scappoose (SPB), heading south towards Salem or Independence, Oregon. We had to wait until 7:35 before getting any responses to our 122.75 calls, when finally we connected with Jim and decided to go to the Flying M. However, before we arrived, several other RV pilots came on the radio and the destination was changed to Woodland, Washington, just a stone's throw across the Columbia River from Scappoose. So we flew back over Scappoose, where we'd started earlier, and went on to Woodland. It didn't matter that we'd just come from Scappoose—we were out to fly.

The skies were gray with intermittent showers. We dodged a few, went through a few, but still enjoyed good flying. There were no winds aloft, so it was a pretty smooth ride across the sun-less sky.

I was the first to land at Woodland. Hank came in second, then Joe, then Jim, and then the rest trickled into the pattern before putting wheels down as well. Starving, we all started to walk to the restaurant to get a table.

We asked the waitress to set up a table for about fifteen, not knowing for sure how many were coming. After we had all ordered and the gab continued, someone mentioned that there were sixteen RV's parked at Woodland. I noticed everybody looked around and did a silent head count, just as I did. So the next question was, did anybody bring a passenger? The answer was surprising—not a single passenger! 16 pilots, 16 RV's. And this was an unplanned gathering.

The food was delicious, the company was great, and I believe there was an unspoken sense of camaraderie amongst the sixteen of us at that table. We shared the RV bond. And, although I enjoy the company of these men immensely, there are times when I still wish there were other women flying with us. I sometimes need a break from men-talk. Occasionally that happens, but today I was alone again with the fifteen men and our gaggle of RV's.

**"RV Gaggle"**
**Photo by: Marcy Lange**

# Best Trip Yet

## Oshkosh 2004

*T*owards the end of July, 2004, it was very hot in the Pacific Northwest. Hank and I were planning to fly to Oshkosh for 'AirVenture' with another airplane, an RV-6 owned and built by Dean and his wife Joy. They were a young couple living in Scappoose and had a hangar at our home airport. We met them at our EAA Chapter 105 and quickly became friends. We'd flown together sometimes along the Willamette Valley, and enjoyed their company. Dean is a computer savvy guy who works for Intel. He's a super nice man and has a nickname that I have no idea where he got—he calls in on the air, saying, 'Quack, quack,' and we all know instantly who it is. Dean is "The Duck". With always a kind word to offer and a great head of knowledge, he's always good company. His wife Joy is also friendly and a lot of fun to be with. She's a slender woman and is still nuts about soccer—she plays in a soccer league and coaches high school soccer. I've enjoyed her company immensely. Both are in their late thirties, very slight and trim of build, with teenagers still at home. We'd talked about making this trip together for a while, and as the time grew near, we began to make a plan.

We decided to start our trip east very early in the morning. This was driven primarily by the intense heat covering most of the country that summer. The earlier we were able to get airborne, the cooler the flight. I don't tolerate heat very well anyway, always dreading the summer humidity, so the early starts would help me significantly. I know 'hot is hot,' but there is a difference between the heat of Oregon and the heat in Wisconsin—humidity levels are much lower in Oregon, so the heat becomes a little more bearable. But we would be flying to Wisconsin, the heat and humidity increasing along the way, and I would need any relief I could get.

We departed Scappoose (SPB) at 4:58 a.m., on July, 24, 2004. The temperature was a reasonable eighty-one degrees. Our first marker was Lewiston, Idaho (LWS). I don't think Joy was overly pleased with the early start, but she adjusted well and I think even got a little nap in after leveling off at altitude. She was in her usual good humor by the time we first stopped. At 5:15 a.m., we cruised past towering Mt. Hood on our right and, looking left, Mt. St. Helens, Mt. Rainier and Mt. Adams. The sun had yet to rise, but there was a promising glow on the horizon. Gradually, a pink semi-circle appeared, growing slowly brighter and brighter until at last the sun broke across the horizon and introduced itself to a new day. It was 5:35 a.m. and I had to reach for my sun glasses—the red sun rising was now shining right into my eyes. Soon Lewiston appeared below, but since it was only a marker, we kept flying east at about 9500 feet.

It was 6:45 a.m. when we started climbing in altitude to cross the peaks of the Rockies. The outside temperature was now forty-eight degrees—finally, some cool air! By 7:00 a.m. I was getting hungry. I'd been up since 3:00 a.m. after not sleeping well, and was struggling a little with my energy. Perhaps it was nerves, perhaps excitement that kept me awake, but I needed nourishment, so I ate an apple and a health bar I had brought along. We flew at 11,500 feet the rest of this leg.

At 7:45 a.m. PST, we landed in Helena, Montana (HLN). The temperature there was sixty-eight degrees. Scappoose to Helena Montana was 550 miles and we covered them in 2 hours and 47 minutes. Our fuel stop was at a FBO called 'Mustang Mickey's', one of the best FBO's in the country. They have several loaner cars for pilots to use and a bunkhouse within the FBO that welcomes weary travelers at no charge. Fuel is purchased, but is as inexpensive as you can find anywhere. They also have a big bathroom complete with a shower and towels and soaps, if you need them. It's one of our favorite stops along the route. We walked around a bit, stretching our legs after fueling, and decided to head out again and cover some more ground while temperatures remained cool.

8:31 a.m. was lift off from Helena. Our next destination was Mandan, North Dakota (Y19), 525 miles from Helena. We climbed to 9500 feet for the cooler air, our speed averaging 185-190 mph. After encountering some clouds we climbed to 11,500 feet. Most of that leg was flown at 11,500 feet because it was beautiful, cool, and smooth flying most of the time. We all enjoyed playing a bit in the clouds, dodging, circling, and having a good time. This leg was so easy and threat-free it became pure joy. As we descended to land at Mandan, it got a little rougher, but nothing too difficult to manage. We touched down at Mandan at 11:30 a.m. PST. The temperature at Mandan was a comfortable seventy-five degrees, the day peaceful and calm.

We were all hungry, so we took the airport loaner car and headed into town for some breakfast. We'd covered almost 1100 miles in just under six hours.

After our late breakfast and return to the FBO, we hung out and rested there for a spell. A pert woman in her fifties came into the FBO and after chatting with her a little while, discovered she was Minnie from 'Mustang Mickey's' in Helena. Then Mickey came in and we were introduced all around. We talked for a while with them, sharing that we had just come from their place in Helena. They were very nice, friendly people.

At 3:45 p.m. CST, we had lift off from Mandan, heading for Minneapolis Crystal (MIC), approximately 382 miles away. While in the air we said our goodbyes to Dean and Joy and continued to Wausau. Dean and Joy were making a stop to visit friends there while we wanted to stop in Wausau to visit some of our family, some long-awaited social time before heading into Oshkosh for the Fly-In. We landed in Wausau at 5:28 p.m. CST.

We spent two days visiting family then headed to Oshkosh for 'AirVenture.'

# Home Alone

## (Just Me and My RV)
## August 2004

### Monday, August 2, 2004

My airplane, the famous plum purple and green RV-6A, was parked in a hanger in Wausau, Wisconsin. An old friend from our Wisconsin EAA Chapter heard we were flying in and generously offered his hangar for the 6A since he was flying his Ercoupe into Oshkosh and his hanger would be empty that week. I didn't plan on flying into Oshkosh with the 6A, but I always enjoy the flight back to the state of my birth and visiting the family and friends that are still there. Anyway, after the RV was tucked away in a solid, insulated hangar, I rented a car and drove the 1.7 hours to Oshkosh.

My flight to Oshkosh, via Wausau, on July 24th, was perhaps the best flight to Wisconsin I've ever made. (That flight is the previous story 'Best Trip Yet'). I attribute most of the success of that trip to the weather; it was perfect all the way. The fun part of the trip was, of course, the people we were with. The temperatures were in the seventies instead of the usual nineties, which meant all of us were still spry and alert after flying three hour legs. We were also able to fly around any looming storm cells, easing the stress on us all. We made that trip in just under nine hours, a good time for the roughly eighteen hundred miles we flew. To drive that route would require close to two thousand miles, and probably two or three days of driving.

Hank lifted off from Oshkosh on Saturday, to fly home in a hurry, as usual, and with only a brief warning of his departure. After spending a quiet but pleasant week in the campground, he had 'sat his limit.' I couldn't leave yet because our Wisconsin camper wasn't packed up and there wasn't enough lead time after he announced he was leaving. I tried to connect with other RVers flying west, to possibly fly home with them, but that didn't work out like it had in the past. I'd flown my 6A to Oshkosh alone many times before, but there were always other RVs along. Hank often made the trip home alone and earlier than the rest of us, so I guess it was time for me to do it alone.

The weather was looking questionable the morning of my departure. It was August 2, 2004. There appeared to be a slim chance that I might be able to get airborne and slide out between two cells moving into Wisconsin, and fearing possible delays if I wait, decided to take the chance. The weather radar indicated I would have clear flying to Mankato, Minnesota, then I'd have to check radar again and make some decisions. If I stayed another day in Wausau, I might be stuck there for two days.

Since my airplane was still nestled in the beautifully equipped Wausau hangar, I spent a day and a half visiting my sister. It was wheels up from Wausau (AUW) at 8:45 a.m. CST. That was a rather late start for a cross county trip, but my stomach wasn't feeling well early that morning. I punched Mankato (MKT) into my GPS. Even as I climbed out, the skies to the west were darkening, but I forged ahead. I couldn't go higher than 3,000 feet and even then, the ceiling was coming down. I was now at 2,500 feet. The elevation there is between 1,200-1,500 feet, which I didn't like that much, and I was not sure about tower locations in the area. Eying a patch of blue sky, I began to guide the 6A higher, climbing for that patch of blue. I circled in that little clearing before climbing higher, to 12,500 feet. I flew at that altitude for a while, between the layers of clouds, peering down to see only solid white, no ground in sight. I flew like that for a while, but was uncomfortable with it. Looking for an opening in the clouds where I could descend, I finally spotted one and took the opportunity to descend. I had to circle while descending, circling so many times I lost count. As I got below the clouds, the skies to the north looked very unfriendly. I was forced to fly south. La Crosse, Wisconsin (LSE) was about fifteen miles ahead so I opted to go there. I had no problem landing there, as the tower gave me a right base clear to land on runway 21, landing gently at 9:45 a.m. I fueled up there, for $3.20 per gallon, and briefly considered heading out again before my wiser-side decided to check the weather again first.

When I checked the weather it indicated there was a storm cell just to the north of us and it looked like I could make it out if I headed south. After five minutes, the skies all around were getting very dark. I decided to stay put until the front passed. When I went out to tie down the 6A I was amazed at how black and ominous the skies had become. But that's standard for the weather in the Midwest—fifteen minutes can make a drastic difference. A guy working the ramp drove up to me and asked if I wanted to put my airplane in a hangar, to wait out the storm. I said, "of course," hoisted myself back into the 6A, and followed him to a cozy looking hangar. By the time the airplane was parked and the hangar doors closed, it was raining. Running back to the FBO I got soaked. Soon thunder and lightning began rocking the area. Thank God my airplane was inside!

By noon the storm had passed and a quick weather check confirmed that I should be able to get farther west that day, possibly as far as Aberdeen, South Dakota (ABR), a mere 369 miles.

It was 12:15 p.m. CST when I departed La Crosse (LSE), immediately climbing to 4500 feet. Flying west, I will usually encounter head winds, but I was cruising at 191 mph, with rpm's at 2200 and manifold pressure at 2200, or about seventy-five percent power. I was burning about seven gph. It was very muggy, the humidity of the Midwest already at the annoying point. I stayed at that altitude, always cruising between 189-195 mph. Earlier that morning I had experienced some lower intestinal aggravation, which was why my departure was somewhat delayed. At 4500 feet, I began feeling it again. I didn't think I would make it to Aberdeen. I picked the closest airport, Montevideo, Minnesota (MVE) and quickly landed there. It was now 1:45 p.m. CST. I spent about twenty minutes there, speaking briefly with a very nice older couple (about my age) who managed the FBO, and stalling departure to see if my intestines would settle down. I checked the weather once more and although there was some rain indicated, it was light sprinkles only, nothing threatening. As I climbed into the 6A, a light drizzle started. The sky was still light though, so I decided to try to outrun the rain.

I departed Montevideo (MVE) at 2:05 p.m. CST, then plugged Dickinson, North Dakota (DIK) into my GPS. I had the drizzle follow me for a few minutes out of Montevideo, but the skies were lighter in the direction of Dickinson, so I continued on. At 3,000 feet I was cruising at 185 mph, at

23 squared, burning 7.5 gallons per hour (gph). I climbed to 4,500 feet and got the same readings. Soon I began to rock and roll a little, bouncing slightly, so I ascended to 6,500 feet. The battering and bouncing continued, but I was cruising at 193 mph, at 22.9 squared, burning 7 gph. I don't like rocking that much, but was confident I could stand it because of the good time and fuel burn I was experiencing. Most of that leg was the same rocking and rolling, so I played with my NAVAID (a form of auto pilot; it keeps the airplane flying steady and straight). Sometimes I find the NAVAID frustrating. No matter how I tweaked it, NAVAID wanted to veer to the left, always taking me left of my course. (I know now that the airplane was slightly out of trim, meaning that slight adjustments to the trim features of the 6A would allow the NAVAID to function perfectly.) However, what I did like was the fact that the wing leveler was better at handling the rocking than I was, so I kept using it. I'd turn it off to correct my course then turn it back on to stabilize the rocking. Although I was bouncing around quite a bit, and the skies were grey, I never felt threatened by the weather.

I landed at Dickinson (DIK) at 4:15 p.m. CST, topped off my fuel tanks at $2.99 per gallon, and checked the weather again. I didn't want to quit flying for the day. Although the weather was bleak and somewhat unpleasant, and although I'd been flying for several hours, I didn't feel stressed or tired. I wanted to get farther west so I could take on the Rocky Mountains early the next morning. The weather was definitely a major concern, but the radar wasn't showing any serious storms. I decided to head for Lewiston, Montana (LWT) or possibly Stanford, Montana (S64). The flight would determine the end destination today.

I departed Dickinson, North Dakota at 5:35 p.m. CST, plugging Lewistown, Montana (LWT) into my GPS. This leg was the most troublesome weather wise. I kept detouring around storm cells, flying much farther than a straight line would have been. There were black skies ahead but I wanted to get as far west as I could. I could always go back. The skies to the south were also black, and soon I began to see lightening in that direction as well. When I got twenty-five miles east of Lewiston, I saw lightening ahead. My first reaction was to turn north where the skies were lighter. But the Hays MOA was in that direction. I turned north and debated with myself about what to do, looking around the skies at my options. By this time north was the only direction I could fly. There was an airport on the other side of the MOA—Havre City, Montana (HVR). I'd been monitoring radio frequency 122.75 and there were some pilots chattering about the weather and their destinations. Apparently they'd been heading for Lewiston too. They announced they were going to get fuel at Havre City, so I decided that was a good option for me as well. I was tired by now and really looking forward to quitting for the day.

Since my lower intestinal distress had quieted down a bit, I didn't want to get it in an uproar again by eating, so I didn't eat anything substantial that day. All I munched on were two health bars and some peanuts I had bought somewhere along the way, and decided early on that I'd avoid the fruit I had also picked up. Liquids consisted of one bottle of water at my La Crosse, Wisconsin stop and I sipped on a second bottle while in route. Breakfast was cancelled because of the stomach aggravation I was experiencing, but I did have a tiny cup of coffee at my sister's place to ward off a caffeine headache.

While flying through the MOA, I prayed again. This is a very long trip and I felt very alone. As I continued my flight to Havre City, I heard on the radio that the other experimentals were landing there too. When I announced my entry to a downwind, the guys on the ground came on the frequency and said if I was looking for fuel I was out of luck. They said they had called Cut Bank, Montana (CTB) and the FBO would be there, adding that he had fuel. So I continued flying and plugged Cut Bank (CTB) into my GPS, turning the nose of my airplane toward lighter skies. Cut Bank was another one hundred miles. The sun was going down and I was one tired old lady. I was definitely going to stop for the day. Soon the other pilots were on the radio again, indicating they too were heading for Cut Bank. I asked what kind of experimentals they were flying, and I heard the reply, "Glassairs, three Glassairs." They were also coming from Oshkosh and heading west to Oregon and Washington.

This part of the long leg was a fairly smooth flight, although I was experiencing a little head wind. The three Glassairs, of course, quickly overtook me, but they only landed a few minutes before I did. As I prepared for my approach, the sun shone through a slight haze and struck me right in my eyes, appearing for the first time that day. I landed at Cut Bank at 8:30 p.m. CST. Two of the Glassairs were factory airplanes and I must admit, all three were handsome airplanes, beautifully built.

I had flown about 7.5 hours, according to my Hobbs meter, but it felt like I'd been in the air for at least 12. The gas was self-serve. After the three Glassairs fueled up, I took my turn. Fuel price was $2.73 per gallon. The FBO was very friendly, offering me use of one of their courtesy cars. I called for a room in town and the first motel was completely booked. The other motel had one room left, so I took it, even though it was a smoking room. After a shower and some vending machine snacks to fend off the pangs of hunger, I felt somewhat human again, but very tired. I slept like a log.

## Tuesday, August 3, 2004

I slept later than usual. After dressing, fixing my hair and driving to the airport, I checked the weather forecast for the day. It looked like it would be very 'iffy' getting across the mountains this morning. I decided to head for Kalispell, Montana, which is a beautiful place to be stuck. I was going to fly through Maria's Pass because the ceiling looked questionable for an attempt going over it. If I had to turn around, I'd have to fly real slow because there wasn't much room to turn the airplane around if I was forced to do so.

I departed Cut Bank at 7:55 a.m. Mountain Standard Time (MST) and plugged Kalispell (S27) into my GPS. Sizing up those mountains ahead led to some trepidation. I sighted Maria's Pass off to my left, but it seemed as though there was just enough room to squeeze between the mountain tops and the clouds. I climbed to 8,500 feet. Visibility was good, although a little murky. The surrounding peaks were jagged and threatening, reaching 9,500 feet into the sky. About 30 miles west of Kalispell the sky ahead became extremely hazy, visibility dropping sharply. Although it was a little scary, I did have options—a road on my left, which was the famous Maria's Pass, or I could turn back. I was flying in pretty much a straight line to Kalispell and I calculated about an hour of flying time for that leg.

As I came over that last peak, the view of the valley below was spectacular. The mountains drop off sharply into a beautiful, lush, green valley complete with a river and scattered habitation. The city itself lay farther south, but the airport was clearly visible, especially the long 3,600 foot by 60 foot runway. Kalispell is a large airport that can be seen from quite a distance. The tower cleared me to make a long final approach—straight in—just like the big boys. Flying a normal airport pattern to land an airplane gave me time to make adjustments to my landing criteria. Factors such as the airspeed and proper altitude required adjustment, but it also gave the other pilots notification of my exact position. I don't ever remember doing a 'straight in' before, so I focused hard on getting it right. Everything went as intended, smooth and error-free. I landed at 8:40 a.m. MST. The elevation at Kalispell is 2,932 feet.

Edwards Jet Center treated me like royalty. They even gave me a ride to the Jet Center in a ramp cart. (That was a first) The Jet Center is new and gorgeous, with many accommodations and a staff of friendly people. If I had to be stuck someplace because of bad weather, this would be the place. As I gazed towards the west, I noticed the weather in that direction was not looking good and there was light rain falling now here in Kalispell. I hung out there for a few hours, prior to getting another weather briefing and inquiring into conditions in Lewiston, Idaho. There was a storm cell moving in that direction, but to the south of Lewiston it was reported to be clear. Taking a moment, I walked around outside and although it was sprinkling a bit, I could see very light skies to the south. Looking due west the sky was very dark and threatening. I decided if I didn't make an attempt to get south I'd be stranded there a day or two, so I opted to take the chance.

I departed Kalispell at 11:30 a.m. MST, after fueling up at $3.14 per gallon. There was a light drizzle, but it appeared very promising to the south. Hoping to fly around the storm cell moving into Lewiston, I flew in light drizzle for around five minutes before my route carried me to open sky and a re-emerging sun. Much to my surprise, flying over Flathead Lake was like a glide, smooth and even. I headed for Missoula, then continued south past Hamilton, Montana. I could see the tops of the mountains, the steepest peaks to the west rising to about 8,000 feet, and there seemed to be just enough of a clearing to skim the tops of the mountains and yet remain under the clouds. I flew a little bit south of Hamilton, then made a sharp right turn toward the west. In my weather briefing, I had asked about conditions in Baker City and Pendleton, Oregon, just over the Idaho border. Knowing there were clear skies there, I just had to fly over these last ridges before clearing the worst of the weather.

The clouds were not solid, but I had to climb over a few to stay heading due west. My altitude varied from 10,500 to 12,500 feet, depending on the clouds. As I flew below, above and around these clouds, I was in awe. They looked so soft, so close, I felt I could reach out and touch them, feeling the softness of cotton balls scattered over the mountain tops. The only thing I was missing was the appropriate music to accompany the beauty.

Too often, we forget to appreciate the beauty around us and the freedom we take for granted. Where else in the world do average citizens like me have the opportunity to do what I was doing? I have flown across this country many times and I've driven across it often as well, and always, at some point along the way, I think about what a privilege it is to have the freedom to do that. After 9/11, these freedoms are especially precious.

It was fairly smooth flying over and around the clouds that were hovering around these peaks, but that was short lived. When I finally passed the last peak, the ground below dropped to about 6,000 feet and was relatively flat. The winds were howling and I began to rock and roll. Man, was it rough! I really didn't want to go to Pendleton, so I plugged Hermiston, Oregon (HRI) into my GPS. I could see it was clear skies ahead so I hung on and surged ahead, slowing the plane down as needed to combat a fairly stiff headwind. Having escaped serious headwinds thus far, I began to feel this leg would make up for their absence. Even though there was a strong crosswind, about twenty knots gusting to twenty-five, I managed a safe landing at Hermiston about 1:50 p.m. MST.

I could almost see home. I could feel it. The Cascade Mountains lay between me and home. I was back in Oregon and I'd almost completed this awesome trip. Checking the weather again, I learned there were plenty of clouds and lots of wind. I hung out at Hermiston for a bit, but I was restless. I could have waited until evening, when the winds would die down, but I knew the flight to Scappoose, my home airport, was only a little over an hour, even if the winds were strong.

I decided to grit my teeth, tighten my safety harness, and head home. I departed Hermiston at 2:20 p.m. PST. The first thing I had to do was avoid the Boardman MOA, so I skirted the northeast corner of it and flew over Washington state before climbing to 6,500 feet. The winds still howled, but the skies were blue and clear, except for the Cascades ahead. There I could see some clouds hanging over them, but thought if I couldn't get under them I still had the option of flying through the Columbia Gorge, or climbing over the clouds. It was rough going, indeed. I'm not talking about rocking and rolling rough—I'm talking about almost tumbling-out-of-the-sky rough. I climbed to 8,500 feet and continued flying west. Still rough, I hung on with all I had. As I approached the Cascades, I had to climb again to 10,500 feet to get over the thick clouds hugging their peaks. 'No problem,' I thought to myself, 'I fly an RV!'

When I was finally over the last of the peaks and could see the valley we live in below, I became overjoyed. The excitement I felt inside was new to me. Or maybe it was nausea; in any case, I was very excited. Scappoose is 58 feet above sea level, so descending from 10,500 feet was another circling game, round and round, down and down, over and over again. But I was almost home. I circled at least a dozen times to loose altitude, my engine still purring like a contented cat, although I had to watch my cylinder head temperatures because they were cooling pretty fast. My excitement grew. I thought it would be a nice surprise to just show up at home, so I landed at Scappoose at 3:30 p.m. PST and didn't say a word.

I was ecstatic and proud. I had made it, flying close to 2,000 miles by myself, without another airplane accompanying me and with miserable weather confronting me throughout. The total trip time, according to my Hobbs meter, was 11.4 hours. Since landing safely at my home airport, I've asked myself if I would do it again, and honestly, I don't think I would. Unless I was forced to. It was not a fun trip, like the trip to Oshkosh had been fun; it was merely a trip that needed to be done. I'm glad I made the flight because it was a confidence booster and a demonstration of courage, something we all wonder if we have inside when we need it. I also recognized that perhaps I'm a little spoiled, having grown so accustomed to flying with other RV's, but it is a vastly more enjoyable experience when there is another airplane along.

**"Me & My RV"**
**Photo by: Mark Sandstrom**

# Karly

## April 2007

*I*t was supposed to be a beautiful, calm day in Wisconsin. Since moving back to Wisconsin in 2005, I've attempted to take my grandkids flying whenever opportunities arose and the weather managed to cooperate. I always wanted them to have a pleasant flying experience. But Wisconsin, like most of the Midwest, has unpredictable weather. It can change quite fast.

This particular morning I was going to take one of my granddaughters, Karly, age seven, flying with me. I picked her up and we drove to the airport, got the airplane out of the hangar, did the pre-flight routine, and then fueled up. We were ready to fly.

Karly is the cutest seven year old. She has the prettiest color of hair that I've ever seen, her long tresses a nice shade of red and blonde, with her eyes a lovely shade of blue. Her cute little nose has a ski jump on the end. I find it strange that she's one of very few redheads I've ever known that can wear any color and still look good. She's tall for her age, and lean, but shows strength in all her physical activities. She's all girl—she loves to wear skirts and girly clothes and has varied moods, like most girls. Today she was chatty and not a bit moody.

The most amazing, the most scenic flights I can remember from my years in Oregon were the flights to the ocean. In early spring one year we flew out to the coast to have breakfast, then some of the men were going to go whale watching. To do this, they would have to fly perhaps a mile or more out to sea and then look for the whales. That sounded very exciting, so Hank and I went along. However, I was too chicken to fly more than a half mile off shore, so I missed seeing any whales that day. The view inland, however, was breath taking. Many of those ocean flights remain as vivid memories for me.

For some reason, I thought of those flights this morning and thought, 'Hey, we have Lake Michigan.' I knew there would be no whales to spot, but flying over a great expanse of water again, that sounded inviting. So, after lifting off from a small airstrip outside of Madison, Wisconsin, I turned the airplane east and headed for the big lake. Flight time to the lake was about a half hour and during that time Karly and I chatted a bit about her school and what she was interested in, and whether or not she was looking forward to going back to school after the break. The lake was soon in view and I asked Karly if she noticed anything, but she didn't comment. Persisting, I asked her if she knew what that large body of water was, and she said, "Isn't that Lake Michigan?" I told her, "Sure is."

By this time I was quite a bit north of Milwaukee's airspace. Ideally, I'd prefer to fly south along the shore, so Karly could easily see the scenic shoreline on her right, but that would have taken me back towards Milwaukee's airspace. I settled for heading north. Karly couldn't see the coastline as well as I could, but I kept tipping the wing so she'd see the sandy beaches and green water below. The only difference from the Pacific Coast flight is the color of the ocean, the Pacific being a deep blue while Lake Michigan presents an emerald green. I'm not sure if Karly appreciated the beauty of it, because at age seven, that's hard to tell. I know I loved the view and the entire flight, as it reminded me so much of the other ocean flights I'd made. I'd asked her several times if she'd like to fly the airplane, but she had declined. She wasn't ready for that.

Just for the fun of it, I did a touch and go at Sheboygan, Wisconsin (SBM), along the Lake Michigan shore, then another touch and go at Manitowoc (MTW). I thought perhaps we'd stop at Sheboygan for a snack, since they have a really nice restaurant there, but it was getting a little windy. I asked Karly if she was okay with the bumps and she said she was fine. It appeared to me, however, that she was a little uncomfortable with the bouncing around.

After 1.8 hours in the air, I decided to call it a day. Our landing was without incident, as we approached the airport in calmer winds. Karly helped me put the airplane back in the hangar before we headed home. That night I couldn't help thinking about the memories made that day with my granddaughter Karly.

# Jared

## July 2007

*I* was in the mood for flying. Saturday's weather was predicted to be a pleasant day, and quite warm. I thought I'd better get to the airport soon and get going before the real heat settled in. I called my daughter to see if Karly or perhaps Jared, my grandkids, would like to go flying with me. She said they were headed up north for a birthday party for a cousin. I said I'd fly one of them up there, if one wanted to, and we could meet shortly at the airport. Jared excitedly agreed to accompany me, so I picked him up and we drove to the airport nearby.

Jared is six years old and a strong little guy, so he was a big help getting the airplane out of the hangar. He's also a redhead, like his sister Karly, but he wears his hair short. His eyes are the same shade of blue as Karly's, but whereas Karly is lean, Jared is built like a Sherman tank. His nature and personality are also much different than Karly's. He's easy going and laid back and the only grandchild I have that is a snuggler. My first memory of him snuggling was when I was babysitting for him, when he was about a year old. He would be on the floor playing with something, then he'd come over by me and lay his head on my lap for fifteen-to-twenty seconds then go back to his playing. He'd do that every so often while he played, just come over for a hug or put his head on my lap. He's always ready to give someone a hug.

We did the pre-flight routine and then crawled into the airplane and taxied over to the run-up area. We had plenty of fuel. I lifted off and headed north into a clear and calm sky, where light, feathery clouds were scattered about. I pointed out a few landmarks to Jared as we passed them. When I asked Jared if he wanted to fly the airplane, he said, "No, that's okay." Most kids take that opportunity to fly the airplane, but my grandkids didn't want to do that, not yet anyway. He simply enjoyed looking around. About forty minutes later we landed at Central Wisconsin Airport (CWA), near Wausau, where we met his parents. Jared had a party to go to. I began thinking about that, wondering to myself, 'How many six year olds arrive at a birthday party in an airplane flown by their Grandma?'

## October 2010

It was Sunday, and the weather had been fairly breezy all weekend. I wanted to get my flying fix, but the weather wouldn't seem to cooperate. Late in the day, the winds quieted down and I still wanted to fly, so I called my daughter and asked if one of the kids wanted to go for a short flight. (My oldest daughter will not fly with me, or anyone. She likes her feet planted on the ground.) Jared was game for flight, so I picked him up and we drove to the airport. It would have to be a short flight, but if I timed it right, it would be perfect.

As we pulled the airplane out of the hangar I realized how big and strong Jared was getting. He could have pulled that airplane out by himself, except he needed me to steer it. Jared is now nine years old and a big boy for his age. He still has the build of a Sherman tank. We did our pre-flight routine, then hopped in the airplane. I purposely headed east. It was indeed calm now, not a breeze or bump in the sky. The air was like glass, offering a flight that rode smooth as silk. I asked Jared if he wanted to fly the airplane, and again he said, "No, that's okay." In all of the one hundred and twenty Young Eagle flights I've given, there's only been a handful of kids that have not wanted to fly the airplane. It's more common for them to want to experience that sense of control. But my grandkids don't want to fly the airplane, though I'm sure they enjoy the flying. Strange. I would have been eager to take the stick and fly an airplane at that age.

Well, we flew along for a bit with that east heading. I kept glancing back to watch the sun setting and hoping I could time it just right. Finally, I decided it was time. I turned the airplane around and we flew directly toward the descending sun. It was a very large, red and orange ball sitting on the horizon. We continued flying west, keeping eyes fixed on the horizon now turning to brilliant tints of orange and red and purple. As I had hoped, we watched the sun set, then did a left base to land. There was only a hint of light left in the sky as we put wheels back to ground. It was a perfect landing to a short flight, one I'll recall later as 'Oh so sweet!'

I sure appreciate the help from Jared pushing that airplane back into the hangar. It's an uphill struggle, but his strength gets the task done. It's only one of the reasons I love having him along.

# Ralph

## September 2007

*I* recently attended a birthday party for a dear friend of mine, Ralph, in Wausau. Actually, his wife Elnora was more my friend than Ralph, but he was around a lot too, especially after he retired. Once retired, he spent much more time with his wife, and that's how I got to know him better. He's a quiet guy, who always has kind words, smiles a lot, laughs often, and seems to adore his wife (so he gets lots of extra points there). I guess I never really knew him, nor did I ever take the time to know him, which I now regret.

I was looking forward to what was supposed to be a beautiful weekend. Since there wasn't much going on with fly-in breakfasts around here, I called Ralph and Elnora and asked if they were free for breakfast and maybe an airplane ride if they were up to it. I knew Ralph was a pilot in his younger years, although we never had much of a conversation about flying before. In defense of my 'lack of interest' in discussing flying with Ralph, I knew them long before I ever met my pilot husband, and got interested in flying myself. When I first got to know them, Ralph's wife and I were interested in horses and spent many a summer days riding the trails around our farm, 'Evergreen Acres.'

Anyway, I flew up to Wausau, where Ralph and Elnora live, and I took them for rides in the 6A before breakfast. Ralph climbed into my airplane and away we flew. We took an air tour of Wausau, then around the countryside. I asked Ralph if he wanted to fly the plane, so he took the stick. He was surprised at how light the controls were. There's a huge difference flying the RVs from most commercially built airplanes. At least the home built airplanes I've flown were all very light on the controls, very easy to fly. Ralph enjoyed the flight and when we landed he was all smiles.

The next ride was with Elnora, and she thoroughly enjoyed the ride too, although she wasn't interested in flying the airplane herself. After I'd given Elnora a tour of the countryside, we glided back to the airport, where Ralph was waiting for us.

Conversation over breakfast revealed that Ralph had a birthday coming up. I knew they were a little older than me; they were older when I first met them some thirty-five years ago. Well, Ralph was turning ninety years young in February, which meant Elnora was eighty-eight. I was shocked beyond speech. These two old timers are almost as spry as I remember them when we went horseback riding in the 1970's. Ralph is still skiing, playing tennis, and doing water aerobics. I'll bet there are a few other things he does to stay active I'm unaware of. I'm sure he's slowed down a bit now, but he's still active. Elnora also plays tennis, but I know her game isn't what it used to be because her knees are in bad shape. She also does water aerobics and is still active in charitable organizations. Individually, they are both amazing personalities, who, after nearly seventy years together, still love each other dearly and still find plenty of time to laugh.

I went to Ralph's ninetieth birthday party, rearranging my work schedule so I could take the day off and drive up to Wausau to attend. Ralph was surprised, to say the least. Their three kids and Elnora planned this party and they had three huge display boards of pictures and old news articles about Ralph. One of them was dedicated to his love of flying. He was a Major in the US Air Force and flew fighters during World War II. I'll bet he has many stories about his war flying. I stood there reading that board about his military service, his flying career, the different airplanes he flew and owned, (he favored Bonanzas), and I felt quite ashamed of myself for not knowing any of this before. Here's this quiet man, who never spoke about himself, and was always loving and attentive to his wife and children, was a war hero, a great man, really, who came home from the war to head a major manufacturing company in Wisconsin.

I decided I would need to take more time in the future to 'smell the roses' and truly appreciate the people I call 'friends.'

# Pancake Breakfast in Oshkosh

## May 2009

*I*t was Saturday morning and I was 'chomping on the bit' to go flying. (a phrase I used when the horses would chomp down on their bridle bit when anxious to get going, an indicator for them that soon they'd be out on the trail.) Most pilots know the feeling. A pre-arranged meet-up with my friend Christy and we were heading for the airport, in spite of the overcast skies. Weather was supposed to be 'rain free', so we took a chance.

Christy is a good friend I met in the 99s. (99s—organization of women pilots) She's a chemist by trade and supports herself in her trade. She is also a current CFI and still has students she's giving flight instruction to part-time. She is also IFR certified. Christy is tall and lean, a pretty girl with long brown hair. She's about half my age, about six inches taller than me, but we seem to enjoy this love of flying we have in common and I love to have her sitting right seat. We've been on many adventurous flights together before.

It was Christy's choice to go to Oshkosh for their pancake breakfast. I told her I'd been there for their breakfast two years ago, and it was a huge disappointment. They were trying to scramble eggs in a crock pot. Can you imagine how long that took? In spite of the time it took to cook the eggs, they still weren't quite done. But, with my friend along, I was willing to give them another chance. After all, Oshkosh is the place to be, right?

After liftoff, Christy flew us there. This was the first time I've flown with a non-RV pilot and I was comfortable letting her take complete control. She's an excellent pilot and has great hands. The first thing I tell my passenger when I give them the controls of my RV (though I always keep my hand on the stick) is to *not* do anything suddenly. The RV is extremely light on the controls and responds instantly to any move. After acknowledging that, Christy took over and flew us to Oshkosh. She didn't land it there because she had not landed an RV before, so I took over the controls and we managed an easy enough touchdown.

The Oshkosh breakfast was not an experience I wanted to have again, since rubber pancakes requiring a steak knife to cut and flavorless sausages didn't agree with my palette, nor Christy's. We ate scantily and moved on.

They had a display of a Light Sport airplane in the hangar, and we went over to take a look at it. I don't remember what it was, but it was a nice looking airplane. We chatted with the owner for a little while, and two other RV pilots joined us in the conversation. I rarely encounter RV's in Wisconsin, so it was kind of fun to chat with them. I believe looking at the Light Sport airplane and chatting with the RV guys was the highlight of the breakfast.

After getting clearance to depart Oshkosh, Christy took over the controls again and flew us home. I let her land the RV, with my hand on the stick. It was an excellent landing! She did everything perfectly. I don't want to admit how many landings I made in the 6A before I finally got a good one. The day was another air adventure to be logged with a safe landing ending.

# The Six State Sandwich

## March 2011

My adult mentor and best friend throughout most of my life is my older sister Claudette (Claudie to family). Although growing up I didn't realize how great a person she was, I grew to appreciate her as I became an adult and parent. She now lives in North Carolina, in a small town near Raleigh. Christy, my friend from the previous story, has a good friend in North Carolina too, so we planned to fly the RV-6A to North Carolina for a visit. Spring break allowed me enough time for the trip and Christy had some vacation time left, so we made a plan.

Preparing an airplane for a long cross country flight is an undertaking that seems to only breed stress. In the past, I've flown the 6A from the Oregon coast to Wisconsin and back many times, but I haven't flown a long distance flight like that since I flew the 6A back to Wisconsin, back in early 2006. Since I hadn't flown the 6A all winter, I wanted my mechanic to check it over. My hangar faces north, which presents a problem. In the past my hangar has always been snowed and iced in, and I've been unable to get the hangar doors open until late April, sometimes May. So I called the FBO, in late February, and asked about getting someone to get my hangar open. He's a great guy, always willing to help us pilots. He said he couldn't do it because of a shot rotator cuff in his shoulder, although he said he'd look at it. He called me back in early March to say he had the doors open, but if we got any more snow or freezing rain I'd have to do it myself.

As expected, we got more snow and freezing rain and cold temperatures. On March 12th, I went up to the airport and had to shovel the doors clear. I got one door open, but the steel rod that slides thru two brackets and then into a hole in the concrete, to hold the middle of the doors steady, was frozen below ground level. I couldn't get that door open. So I poured salt in the hole around the steel rod and in front of the doors, hoping we'd get some warmer temperatures and it would thaw the whole area. It did warm up and several days later I got the airplane out, flew it over to my mechanic, and left it there for him to check over.

On Thursday, March 24th, two days before our intended departure to North Carolina, Christy drove me over to get the airplane and I flew it back to my hangar so we could do the final preparations in my hangar. After a comedy of errors involving keys, all my fault, we finally left the airport at 9:30 p.m., long after the sun had gone down.

Our plan was to lift off right before sunrise on Saturday, March 26th. Weather in Wisconsin was cold but clear. There was weather moving into the Raleigh area in the afternoon, so we had a narrow window of time to get in before the weather. If we left from Madison early Saturday morning, we should be there around 12 to 1 o'clock in the afternoon. We were game to try it.

Christy arrived at my house at 6:00 a.m. as planned and we drove to the airport, a nice half hour drive. The temperature was 18 degrees. There was an apron of ice in front of the doors, not from snow but from the freezing rain the area experienced most of the week. The first problem we encountered was the locks were all frozen, gobs of ice hanging from them. I could chip most of it away, but there was ice down in the locks too. Fortunately, Christy had purchased some lock deicer, and after applying that, we got the locks to open. The airplane was finally rolled out, packed, and after a quick visit to the restroom, we both hopped in the plane and started her up.

By the time we got the hangar doors open and in the airplane, ready to go, both Christy and I had frozen fingers. Lift off was at 7:24 a.m., the temperature was 18 degrees. Our destination was the Fuquay/Angier Airport, North Carolina, approximately 705 miles to the southeast. We planned one fuel stop in Ashland, Kentucky, roughly 450 miles from my hangar in Madison. I started flying while Christy called Madison and followed our path on the maps. The weather was mostly clear, some puffy clouds could be seen in our heading, but nothing to worry about. I got the airplane set up to fly 23 squared, manifold pressure at 2,300 and rpm's at 2,300 (that's about seventy-five percent power on the 6A). We climbed to 3,500 feet and only managed an airspeed of 157 mph. Normally, those settings in the 6A will achieve about 185-190 mph. We passed over Joliet, Illinois at 8:25 a.m. and Anderson, Indiana at 9:35 a.m. We managed 145 mph there, burning approximately 7.2 gallons per hour. That's not good news. Obviously we had some strong headwinds and the temperature was very cold. My oil temperature never came up above 54 degrees centigrade. I realized I hadn't checked the oil weight and thought the cold oil temperature was the result of an all season weighted oil, when it should have been a colder temperature oil. The left side of my body was freezing from the waist down. There is only one heater in the 6A and it's located on the far right side, by Christy's feet. But the engine was purring like a lap cat on a cold winter's night, so we continued on.

We had sunshine all the way, in spite of the cold, or because of the cold. We landed at Ashland, Kentucky (DWU) at 11:00 a.m., or 3.4 hrs. after lift-off from Madison. That's a long sit. We fueled up, checked the weather, made a potty stop and climbed back in the airplane. (I did not get warm during this stop) As for weather up ahead, it was looking questionable. We had some mountains to cross.

We lifted off from Ashland at 11:38 a.m. We knew we'd have to go over the Appalachian Mountains, with rolling peaks about 4,500 feet in elevation, so we started the climb. We got to 7,500 feet and began cruising at 178 mph, burning 7.5 gallons per hour (gph). It was a little bumpy up there but we had no choice. We knew the clouds were hugging the mountains so our only hope was to fly over the clouds and find a hole to get down through. We had beautiful sunshine, and that was enough to give us some warmth, although only from the waist up on my side. The clouds kept rising too and we ended up at 11,500 feet. The GPS told us we were above a small private strip called Ferrell, which was in West Virginia. This point was approximately one hour flight time from our destination in Raleigh. The cloud cover was solid here and we knew it was all the way to the ground.

I was suddenly in the clouds and I started to turn around. We were descending slightly in the turn and I hesitated, trying to figure out why. I was thinking about how to react when Christy took the stick, leveled us off and pretty soon we were in blue skies again. It's really nice to have a CFI with lots of IFR experience on board, and Christy's the best. At this point we decided we weren't going to make it, so we headed back to Ashland. We talked about options, knowing we couldn't get to Fuquay/Angier airport sneaking under the clouds and didn't want to get stuck someplace for two or three days, so we decided to head back home to Madison.

We wanted to keep flying as long as we could, but we were both hungry. I hadn't eaten anything yet, and Christy confessed she'd only had a granola bar before she left her house. I had half a cup of coffee at Ashland, Kentucky that the FBO generously made, especially for me. I would have had more because it was good coffee and I usually have one or two cups in the morning, but not knowing how long we'd be in the airplane yet, I was hesitant to consume too much liquid. As we were getting close to Ashland, we decided we'd been there before and wanted to stop at a different airport. So we headed for a promising sounding airport along the way, in Middletown, Ohio (MWO). Our EAA Chapter in Wisconsin is based in Middleton, Wisconsin.

We landed at Middletown, Ohio at 1:50 p.m., after about 2.2 hours of air time. We fueled up again and the FBO offered to drive us to the end of the runway, where we got out and crossed a street to where a Marc's Big Boy restaurant waited. It was too late for breakfast, so we were forced to order sandwiches. Christy nibbled on her sandwich, while I inhaled mine. Looking at us, it's obvious who the nibbler is and who's the inhaler. We got picked up again by the FBO at the end of the runway and, after checking weather and making a final potty stop, we climbed in the 6A.

There was snow predicted at Middletown for the evening, so getting airborne quickly was critical. Lift off from MWO was 3:08 p.m. We had seventeen knot winds and the temperature was cold. We climbed to 4,500 feet, cruising at 177-188 mph, burning 7.2 gph. The airspeed was constantly changing so we knew we had some strong winds outside; however, the ride was not that bumpy, so we continued on. It was now overcast, hazy, and there was rain and snow predicted ahead. We were just south of Madison, around 5:20 p.m., when we encountered rain. Or was it snow? It was hard to tell, but my guess was sleet. We kept an eye on the leading edges of the wings for icing, a dangerous development, but saw none.

Christy was doing the flying for the entire leg while I was doing the watching and map work. Believe me when I say that our chances of getting past Madison looked bleak. We descended to 2,200 feet, to stay below Madison's airspace, and continued on. (We didn't want to talk to them this time). There were heavy showers all around us. Christy detoured slightly to get around the darkest skies, and just north of Madison the skies opened up and we were suddenly bathed in blue skies. My left side was frozen from the waist down. My right foot and my right side was fine, but my left foot and left side was frozen. I had almost no feeling in my left foot, but we could almost see the hangar now and I knew we'd make it back soon. I'd be able to start thawing shortly!

We landed at my home airport at 5:40 p.m. CST, with the temperature outside lingering at 28 degrees. Flight time was 2.5 hours. We were safe, we were on solid ground, and although we didn't make it to our destination in North Carolina, it was a good experience we were able to share together. We'll attempt this trip again when the weather warms up.

Total flying time was 8.1 hours and approximately 1,200 miles of ground was covered. That's not good time in the RV, but considering the headwinds and the weather, it was reasonable. I'm sure we will make better time in better weather. As the title suggests, we flew over six states—Wisconsin, Illinois, Indiana, Ohio, Kentucky, and West Virginia—and only got a sandwich. I will not admit how much that sandwich cost!

Follow-up: Three hours after I was home, sitting in my living room with the fireplace on and wearing my Cuddle Duds (long underwear) and sweat pants with a blanket over my lap, I was still cold on my left side. I was too tired and too lazy to take a hot bath, so I got the heating pad out and applied it to the left side of my rear. I don't know exactly when I warmed up because I was sleeping long before that occurred. Upon awaking Sunday morning, I was warm. Finally.

**"Christy & Marcy"**
**Photo By: Christy**

# A Hot Saturday In July

## Summer 2011

riday, July 8th, 2011 was hot and humid, 89 degree and a little uncomfortable. I wanted to go flying on Saturday, to satisfy my flying addiction, and since Saturday was going to be hotter and muggier than Friday, I planned to be at the airport early Saturday morning, by 6:00 a.m., and hopefully lift off by 6:15. This summer I'm only doing volunteer work and haven't set an alarm since school let out in June. So I set the alarm for 5:30 a.m. (without my glasses on) and didn't realize I'd set it for 5:30 p.m. instead of a.m. When I woke up at 6:15, I was confused. Why didn't my alarm go off? (I didn't figure it out until after my flying)

Anyway, I brushed my teeth, got dressed, and drove to the airport. To my dismay, I wasn't going anywhere until I put gas in my car, so that was a slight delay. Then, when I got to the airport, I needed to put gas in the airplane, another slight delay. An expensive beginning, but I would not be discouraged. It's about a twenty-five to thirty minute drive to my hangar, so I didn't actually lift off until around 7:30 a.m.

My EAA Chapter was giving Young Eagle rides at Morey's Airport (C29), in Middleton, Wisconsin, so I flew over there to see if anybody was around. I didn't land because there wasn't any activity there yet, and I hadn't really planned to give Young Eagle rides because of the heat. So I turned around and headed north. I had looked for a pancake breakfast but there was none until Sunday, so with no place in particular to go, I decided to work on my quest to land at every airport in Wisconsin. I had Baraboo (DLL) on my nose, so I did a touch and go there, even though I've been in Baraboo before. I was just having fun flying and it was along my route. (Middleton to Baraboo is thirty air miles.) Then I continued my north heading and landed at Adams-Friendship airport (63C). (Baraboo to Adams-Friendship is thirty air miles too) It looks like a nice airport, but at 8:00 a.m. there was no sign of an airplane on the ground or in the air. I didn't see another airplane while I was flying, nor did I hear any chatter on the radio, except for some landings at Sheboygan, along Lake Michigan's shore.

The air at 3,000 feet was warming up. If I'd have climbed a little it may have been cooler, but with the hot summer we'd had so far, I doubted it would be much cooler and for the touch and goes I was doing it seemed more prudent to stay between 2,000 and 3,000 feet. (You burn much more fuel on take offs and landings than on cruise flights.) The skies ahead and below had a greenish tinge to it, with visibility okay but certainly not like it is on a cooler day.

From Adams-Friendship I decided to go to Wautoma (Y50), another small Wisconsin town. Adams-Friendship to Wautoma is twenty-five air miles. Wautoma looks like a nice airport too and I'll have to watch for a breakfast there in the future. I thought of landing at West Bend (2T5) next, so I headed that way. After about twenty-five miles heading southeast to West Bend, I was getting very uncomfortable with the heat and humidity. I decided to head back to my hangar, about twenty-five miles to the west. It was already

87 degrees and growing very muggy. By the time I landed and pushed the plane back into the hangar, I was huffing and puffing and dripping sweat from every part of me. The humidity was obnoxious and I was glad I'd gotten aloft as early as I had.

I flew 1.2 hours, made four touch and goes, and covered approximately 165 air miles. My fuel burn was about 7.5 gph at a power setting of about seventy-five percent. That's a little more than a normal hour of flying, but with all the landings and take offs, that's still not too bad.

# 10 Minutes . . . Or Not

## October 2011

*W*hat do you do when you find you have to get your airplane back home from being serviced and the weather has been nothing but windy? I'm referring to thirty-to-forty knot winds on the ground, with gusts and wind shear at frightening speeds. I was relieved that my mechanic could keep the airplane in his hangar, but I also knew he was just being nice and that he had other planes on the ramp that needed to be brought inside to work on. So, after three days of planning to get my RV home and after failing each day to do so, because of the terrible winds, I made a final plan.

On Monday, October 17[th,] my friend Dave, from my EAA Chapter, was going to pick me up in his airplane at my hangar and fly me over to the mechanic, some forty miles away as the crow flies. By the time I got off work, it was 12:30 p.m. I drove to my hangar and met Dave. Dave is a great guy, in his fifties, about five foot, seven inches tall, with brown hair. He's helped me several times with the airplane, and I've helped him several times too. On one occasion, after he had rotator cuff surgery on his shoulder, he called me and asked if I would take him flying, in his airplane. I said sure, and drove over to his hangar, where he briefed me on flying his Cherokee. It was a fun and easy plane to fly, a 'sweet ride.'

Winds were being reported at fifteen-to-twenty knots on the ground, with some gusting. 'Not too bad,' I thought. That forty mile flight would normally take me approximately ten minutes, but this flight over there was sneaking up on an hour in Dave's Cherokee, with top speed at about 125 mph. He reported tracking 73 mph on our flight over and I was already nervous flying with him at 73 mph and rocking around. The Cherokee is quite a bit heavier than my 6A, by several hundred pounds.

I could tell by the time we got the RV outside that the winds had picked up some more. I didn't check the weather, because it was a ten minute flight back to my own hangar, probably less with the winds in my favor. There were clouds but no rain threat. It wouldn't have made a difference anyway because I just wanted to get the airplane home, and what's ten minutes of bumps?

I got in the 6A and took off, taking a course directly into the wind. I could tell the winds had picked up considerably because when I tried to turn the RV 180 degrees, to head back to my home airport, it took me several miles of an extremely gradual turn to get the plane heading south. It was quite a struggle to keep it level. Already, I was bouncing around up there and feeling nervous. Actually, I was getting scared. I could literally feel the wind pushing me around.

I was so busy hanging on to that stick and dialing down the power settings that I never even looked at the airspeed. I was going too fast, very easy to see and feel at 1,000 feet above the ground. I could feel the speed, not exactly what you want in those conditions. I never glanced at the airspeed indicator because I was too busy keeping the airplane flying level, dialing down power settings, and just hanging on.

Flying at 1,900 feet, I started to set up for the approach pattern. I thought perhaps I'd have trouble making that turn again to land into the wind and I sort of misjudged my turning time. I was on the downwind leg at 1,800 feet when I glanced at the GPS and did a double take. It was reading 283 mph! Shit! I glanced at my power setting—manifold pressure was at 1,500 already and prop setting at 1,600, almost squared, which are almost ideal settings for landing. But I wasn't slowing down!

I dialed down the power settings some more. It took me forever to make that turn and when I finally got it turned around, I thought I should be on a long final approach. But I couldn't see the runways, or the airport for that matter. How confusing! How frightening! I must have grossly misjudged my turn time, or was pushed so far that I lost sight of the airport. My knuckles were white. I was flying strictly by feel and trying to slow the plane down and keep it from flipping. The wind was rocking and rolling me sideways and back. Finally, I saw the runways ahead and started descending. In spite of the fact that I was almost heading directly into that strong headwind, the descent kept adding speed. I was actually idling for a while, with the power settings almost off, crabbing it, and trying to slow it down. I knew I couldn't put my flaps down because I was still around 130 mph. Yes, it was a long final approach. I still had time to slow it down though. By the time I had the runway made, I was still at 100 mph.

The wind was a strong right quartering, so I concentrated on landing with the right wing down a little, but at the last minute the wind lifted that right wing up and I felt the left main gear touch. I saw the wing come up and a ground loop seemed eminent. Then it was all feel. I struggled getting that wing down. At least I think that's what I did, it's all still a blur. As the wing eased down, I could feel the right main gear touch. The touchdown was as bad as any I can remember. But the mains were both down and I could finally put the flaps down full. I used every inch of that 2,560 foot runway before finally coming to a stop. (With my constant speed prop I can normally lift off and stop after touchdown in 500-600 feet.) I was shaking badly and it took me a few minutes to catch my breath. I turned the airplane around and taxied to my hangar.

So many things go through your mind in a stressful situation like that. I've heard people comment after a harrowing experience that their life flashed before them. But honestly, I didn't have any flashes like that. I don't think there was time. I think it was because I was so busy dealing with bumps and jerks and keeping the airplane level. Of course, I thought about a go-around, but that decision was a last minute, desperate move, after attempting to land. I was prepared mentally to go around, but the thought of making two more 180 degree turns was more frightening than the prospect of landing hard, or damaging a gear leg. Would I do it again? Absolutely not! Remember, it was supposed to be a ten minute flight. What kind of pilot are you if you can't stand a little wind for ten minutes?

There was a guy at the airport that met me at the hangar. He said the winds were at twenty-five knots gusting to thirty-five knots on the ground. I think what pushed me to 283 mph with my idle settings was a heck of a lot more than thirty-five knot winds. Certainly the winds up top were a lot more than that.

Thirty minutes later, I was in my car driving home, and my hands were still shaking.

You know what they say, 'You've got to get back up on that horse and go again.' I went flying the following

Saturday, October 22nd, and it was perhaps the best flight of the season. I didn't get airborne until around 1:00 p.m. in the afternoon. The winds were light, at about seven knots. I flew up to Wausau, (about fifty minutes) and met an old friend for lunch. The ride up there was a little bumpy at 3,000 feet, typical flying in the afternoon. When I got back in the airplane around five to return home, there was not even a breeze. It was such calm, easy flying that I didn't want to quit yet, so I flew up to Merrill, Wisconsin, then made a hard right turn to buzz an old flying buddy who lived in the countryside. I circled her place three times, and although I felt exhilarated to be alive and up there boring holes in the sky, it was time to head home. The flight back to my hangar was as smooth as glass. Another day in the skies was drawing to a close and there I was, a crazy old woman getting her thrills alone up there in the blue.

# About the Author

**Photo By: Ellie Hussong**

arcy Lange has had several careers during her lifetime and is presently a Professional Driver. Family, a husband and three children, horses and photography occupied much of her early adulthood. When aviation became a part of her life, she bacame involved working on ground crews. She finally began flying herself at the age of 50. She was hooked from then on.

Printed in the United States
By Bookmasters